One Night in Idaho:

The Bryan Kohberger Case and the Hunt for Justice

Sherwood Dobson

Copyright page

All rights reserved. No part of this publication may be reproduced, distributed, or transmitted in any form or by any means, including photocopying, recording, or other electronic or mechanical methods, without the prior written permission of the publisher, except in the case of brief quotations embodied in critical reviews and certain other noncommercial uses permitted by copyright law.

Copyright © Sherwood Dobson, 2025.

Disclaimer page

This book, "One Night in Idaho: The Bryan Kohberger Case and the Hunt for Justice," is a work of nonfiction based on publicly available information, court documents, law enforcement records, media reports, and the Amazon Prime Video documentary "One Night in Idaho: The College Murders." The author has made every effort to ensure accuracy in the presentation of facts and timeline of events.

Bryan Christopher Kohberger has been charged with four counts of first-degree murder and one count of burglary in connection with the deaths of Madison Mogen, Kaylee Goncalves, Xana Kernodle, and Ethan Chapin. As of the publication of this book, Mr. Kohberger has not been convicted of these charges. Under the laws of the United States, he is presumed innocent until proven guilty beyond a reasonable doubt in a court of law. The trial is scheduled for August 2025, and the outcome remains undetermined.

The information contained in this book is derived from publicly available sources including, but not limited to: probable cause affidavits, court filings, police reports, media interviews, news coverage, social media posts, and the aforementioned documentary. The author has not had direct access to sealed court documents, confidential investigative materials, or private communications between the parties involved.

This book is written with the utmost respect for the victims—Madison Mogen, Kaylee Goncalves, Xana Kernodle, and Ethan Chapin—and their families. The author acknowledges their profound loss and the ongoing grief experienced by their loved ones. Every effort has been made to honor their memory while examining the facts of this case.

While the author has made diligent efforts to verify information and present an accurate account of events, some details may be subject to interpretation or may evolve as additional information becomes available through the legal process. Any errors are unintentional, and the author welcomes corrections for future editions.

Nothing in this book should be construed as legal advice or legal opinion. Readers seeking legal information should consult qualified legal professionals.

This work contains references to copyrighted materials used under the doctrine of fair use for purposes of criticism, comment, news reporting, and educational analysis. No copyright infringement is intended.

As this case involves ongoing legal proceedings, some information may change as the trial progresses and new evidence is presented. This book reflects information available as of [Publication Date] and may not include developments that occur after publication.

The author has made efforts to respect the privacy of individuals not directly involved in the public aspects of this case, including surviving roommates, family members, and others who may prefer to remain private.

Table of Contents

Copyright page.. 2
Disclaimer page.. 3
Introduction: A Night That Changed Everything....... 9
Chapter 1: The Victims - Four Lives Cut Short........ 16
    Madison Mogen: The Marketing Student with Big Dreams... 16
    Kaylee Goncalves: The General Studies Senior Planning Her Future.. 18
    Xana Kernodle: The Funnel Cake Entrepreneur with a Heart of Gold... 20
    Ethan Chapin: The Freshman Finding His Place.. 22
    Bonds of Friendship: The Tight-Knit Group...... 24
Chapter 2: November 13, 2022 - The Final Hours.... 29
    Saturday Night in Moscow: Different Paths, Same Destination... 29
    The Sigma Chi Party: Ethan and Xana's Evening Together..33
    Coming Home: The House on King Road After Midnight.. 37
Chapter 3: Horror in the Dark - The Murders Unfold... 44
    Third Floor Terror: Madison and Kaylee's Final Moments.. 45
    The Surviving Witnesses: Dylan and Bethany's Terrifying Night..48
Chapter 4: The Making of a Suspect - Bryan Kohberger's Dark Journey... 54
    Academic Pursuits: From Community College to

DeSales University... 57
Graduate School Ambitions: Why He Chose Criminal Justice... 60

Chapter 5: Red Flags and Warning Signs................ 65
The Reddit Posts: Anonymous Confessions and Dark Thoughts.. 67
Digital Footprints: Online Searches and Amazon Purchases..71

Chapter 6: Seven Weeks of Terror - The Investigation Begins.. 77
Crime Scene Chaos: Securing Evidence at 1122 King Road... 79
Community in Crisis: Fear Grips the University of Idaho.. 83
Social Media Frenzy: Amateur Sleuths and False Accusations... 87

Chapter 7: The Hunt for Justice - Modern Forensics Crack the Case..91
Genetic Genealogy: Revolutionary Science Identifies a Suspect.. 93
Building the Case: Connecting the Evidence to Bryan Kohberger...97
December 30, 2022: The Arrest That Shocked the Nation.. 102

Chapter 8: Trial by Media and Law - The Path to Justice... 105
Legal Maneuvering: Defense Strategies and Prosecution Response.....................................107
The Documentary Phenomenon: "One Night in Idaho" and Media Impact................................ 111
Preparing for Trial: The Case That Will Define

Modern Forensics.. 116
Conclusion: Legacy of a Tragedy - How Four Lives Lost Changed Criminal Justice Forever..................119

Introduction: A Night That Changed Everything

Some stories begin with a single moment that fractures time into before and after. November 13, 2022, was one of those moments for Moscow, Idaho—a quiet college town nestled in the rolling Palouse hills where the most serious crimes typically involved underage drinking citations and parking violations. By dawn that Sunday morning, four University of Idaho students lay dead in their beds, victims of a brutal stabbing attack that would transform this peaceful community into the epicenter of one of America's most captivating murder investigations.

Madison Mogen, 21, was planning to graduate in May with a marketing degree. Kaylee Goncalves, also 21, had already walked across the stage months early and was preparing to move to Texas for a job with an IT company. Xana Kernodle, 20, balanced her studies with running a small funnel cake business that brought joy to local events. Ethan Chapin, 20, was a freshman from Mount Vernon, Washington, still finding his footing in college life and deeply in love with Xana. These weren't just statistics in a crime report—they were young people with futures, families who loved them, and dreams that would never be realized.

The house at 1122 King Road sat on a sloping lot just blocks from campus, its white exterior and black trim making it indistinguishable from dozens of other student rentals in the area. Six students lived there, splitting rent and navigating the typical challenges of young adult life. The three-story layout meant the residents often went days without seeing each other, passing like ships in the night between classes, work, and social commitments. On November 12, this normal college house routine would unknowingly set the stage for unimaginable tragedy.

That Saturday evening played out like countless others before it. Madison and Kaylee spent their night downtown, moving between the Corner Club and the Mad Greek restaurant, their movements captured on security cameras that would later become crucial evidence. They appeared carefree and happy, just two friends enjoying what they didn't know would be their last night out together. Meanwhile, Ethan had come over to spend time with Xana after attending a Sigma Chi fraternity party. The two other roommates, Dylan Mortensen and Bethany Funke, were also home that night, going about their typical weekend routines.

The last known footage of Madison and Kaylee alive shows them at a local food truck at 1:41 AM, ordering their late-night snack and chatting with the vendor. The brief video, which would be viewed millions of times in the weeks that followed, captures two young women who seem entirely at ease with the world. They had no way of knowing that someone had been watching them, studying their routines, and preparing for what would happen just hours later.

By 4 AM, the house on King Road had fallen into the deep quiet that settles over college neighborhoods in the early morning hours. Most students were either sound asleep or just heading home from late-night parties. It was during this window of vulnerability that an intruder entered the house through a sliding glass door on the second floor. What happened next would unfold over approximately 15 minutes, leaving four people dead and two survivors who would carry the trauma of that night for the rest of their lives.

Dylan Mortensen's encounter with the killer would become one of the most chilling details of the entire case. Around 4 AM, she heard what she thought was Kaylee playing with her dog upstairs. Then came sounds she initially dismissed as partying—voices, a thud, crying. When she opened her bedroom door to investigate, she came face to face with a figure dressed in black clothing and a mask, walking toward the kitchen and back exit. The image of that person—described as 5'10" or taller with bushy eyebrows—would haunt her and eventually help identify the killer.

The discovery of the bodies didn't come until nearly eight hours later, when friends arrived at the house concerned that the roommates weren't answering their phones. The 911 call came in at 11:58 AM, reporting an "unconscious individual." By the time first responders arrived, it was clear this was something far worse than anyone had initially imagined. The Latah County Coroner would later determine that all four victims died from multiple stab wounds, and some had defensive injuries suggesting they fought for their lives.

Moscow, a town of about 25,000 people, had recorded just one murder since 2015. The police department, led by Chief

James Fry, suddenly found themselves managing a quadruple homicide that would draw national media attention and resources from across the state and federal government. The Idaho State Police, FBI, and other agencies quickly joined the investigation, bringing expertise in forensic analysis, behavioral profiling, and digital investigation that the local department had never needed before.

The ripple effects were immediate and profound. University of Idaho students began leaving campus in droves, their parents driving hundreds of miles to pick them up rather than let them stay in what now felt like an unsafe environment. Local businesses that catered to students saw dramatic drops in foot traffic. Hardware stores couldn't keep door locks and security cameras in stock. The sense of safety that had defined this small college town evaporated overnight.

As news of the murders spread beyond Moscow, the case quickly captured national attention in ways that surprised even seasoned crime reporters. Social media platforms exploded with amateur investigators, conspiracy theorists, and true crime enthusiasts dissecting every detail. The combination of young, photogenic victims, a mysterious killer, and a small-town setting created the perfect storm for viral interest. TikTok videos analyzing security footage garnered millions of views. Reddit forums dedicated to the case attracted hundreds of thousands of members. The University of Idaho murders became more than a local tragedy—they became a national obsession.

For seven weeks, the investigation consumed not just Moscow but much of the country. Police received thousands of tips, processed hundreds of pieces of evidence, and conducted countless interviews. They released few details publicly, trying to protect the integrity of their investigation while managing intense public pressure for answers. The silence only fueled more speculation and online theories, some of which targeted innocent people and forced police to repeatedly warn against vigilante justice.

The breakthrough came through a combination of traditional detective work and cutting-edge forensic science. A single piece of evidence left at the crime scene—a tan leather knife sheath found next to one of the victims—contained DNA that would eventually lead investigators to Bryan Christopher Kohberger, a 28-year-old criminology PhD student at Washington State University, just eight miles away from the murder scene.

Kohberger's arrest on December 30, 2022, at his parents' home in Pennsylvania, brought relief to Moscow but raised even more unsettling questions. Here was someone who had been studying criminal behavior and investigative techniques while allegedly planning and carrying out the very type of crime he was learning about in his graduate program. The irony was almost too disturbing to comprehend.

This book tells the complete story of that night and its aftermath—from the final hours of four young lives to the sophisticated investigation that brought their alleged killer to justice. It explores not just what happened in the early morning hours of November 13, 2022, but why it happened, how it was solved, and what it means for our understanding of both criminal behavior and modern investigative techniques.

The story of the Idaho murders is ultimately about more than one terrible night. It's about how a single act of violence can shatter multiple communities, how modern technology and forensic science are revolutionizing criminal investigations, and how the pursuit of justice requires both cutting-edge science and old-fashioned detective work. Most importantly, it's about remembering four young people whose lives were cut short and honoring their memory by seeking to understand the truth of what happened to them.

Chapter 1: The Victims - Four Lives Cut Short

They were ordinary college students living extraordinary lives. Madison Mogen, Kaylee Goncalves, Xana Kernodle, and Ethan Chapin had everything ahead of them when a killer's blade ended their dreams on November 13, 2022. These weren't just statistics in a crime report. They were children with loving families, students with bright futures, and friends who made everyone around them better. Understanding who they were, not just how they died, is essential to comprehending the magnitude of what was lost that terrible night in Moscow, Idaho.

Madison Mogen: The Marketing Student with Big Dreams

Madison "Maddie" Mogen embodied the spirit of a young woman who knew exactly where she was headed. At 21, the senior from Coeur d'Alene, Idaho, was weeks away from graduating with her marketing degree when her life was cut short. She had already secured a job lined up in Boise, ready to put her education to work in the real world.

Maddie wasn't just studying marketing, she was living it. At the Mad Greek restaurant in downtown Moscow, where she worked alongside her roommate Xana Kernodle, Maddie used her skills to run the restaurant's social media campaign. Her natural talent for connecting with people shone through in everything she did, from her infectious laugh captured in countless photos to her ability to light up any room she entered.

Family friend Jessie Frost remembered Maddie's love for the color pink and her excitement about moving to Boise after graduation that spring. But perhaps most telling was how Maddie had found her place in the Pi Beta Phi sorority, where she was known for her kindness and genuine care for others. "She was the world to us," her father Ben Mogen said at a December memorial service, words that captured the devastating void her death left behind.

Maddie's relationship with her boyfriend Jake Schriger revealed her capacity for deep, meaningful connections. "Maddie was my best friend," Schriger shared at the memorial. "She was the first person I talked to every morning and the last person I talked to before bed." Their two-year relationship showed the consistency and loyalty that defined so much of Maddie's character.

Her mother, Karen Laramie, has kept Maddie's memory alive by speaking about her daughter in the present tense, refusing to say "was" when describing her. "Madison is absolutely amazing and always has been," Laramie explained in a 2024 interview, showing how love transcends even death. Along with another mother, Laramie founded the Made With Kindness foundation to honor Madison's legacy and help other students, turning grief into purpose.

What makes Maddie's story even more heartbreaking is how close she was to achieving her dreams. The marketing degree she earned posthumously in spring 2023 wasn't just a sympathy gesture from the university. As her father emphasized when accepting the diploma, "She earned all those credits. They didn't just give it to her because they were trying to be nice."

Kaylee Goncalves: The General Studies Senior Planning Her Future

Kaylee Goncalves was the ultimate middle child in a family of five siblings, the one her family called their "defender and protector." At 21, this senior from Rathdrum, Idaho, was majoring in general studies at the College of Letters, Arts and Social Sciences, but her real education came from life itself. Kaylee was what her sister Alivea called "the ultimate go-getter," someone who "constantly wanted an adventure."

What set Kaylee apart was her fearless approach to life. Her family describes her as someone who "didn't hold back on love, fights or life." She was tough and fair, the sibling who fought for justice and made sure everyone was treated right. In a family dynamic where each child had their role, Kaylee was the "fairness fighter," the one who ensured everyone got what they deserved.

Kaylee had big plans stretching far beyond graduation. She was set to take a trip to Europe and had already secured a job in Texas, ready to start the next chapter of her adult life. Her sister emphasized how everything was falling into place: "She had everything going for her, absolutely everything. She had her job lined up. She had worked really hard for it."

As a member of the Alpha Phi sorority, Kaylee found her community and thrived in the social aspects of college life. But she was equally serious about her academics, graduating early to get a head start on her career. The posthumous bachelor's degree in general studies she received at the May 2023 graduation ceremony represented years of hard work and determination.

Her father Steve's words at the graduation captured the family's profound loss: seeing all those graduation photos just highlighted that "they should be here." The ceremony that should have been Kaylee's triumph became a painful reminder of futures that would never unfold.

Kaylee's room on the third floor of the King Road house became the crime scene where she and Maddie were found together. Her parents revealed the heartbreaking detail that Kaylee appeared to have been "completely, totally trapped" in a corner of the room, fighting until the end. The small bedroom was set up so that "you can't get out of that room" once someone entered. "The bed was the entire room," her mother Kristi explained, "could barely open up the door without swiping the foot of the bed."

Xana Kernodle: The Funnel Cake Entrepreneur with a Heart of Gold

Xana Kernodle brought joy wherever she went. The 20-year-old from Post Falls, Idaho, had a smile that could light up any room and an entrepreneurial spirit that impressed everyone who knew her. At her high school graduation in 2020, she decorated her mortarboard with flowers, butterflies, and the prophetic words: "For The Lives That I Will Change."

Xana was living that motto every day. She worked at the Mad Greek restaurant with her roommate and friend Maddie Mogen, but her true passion project was her funnel cake business. This wasn't just a side hustle for spending money – Xana was building something meaningful, showing the same entrepreneurial drive that would have taken her far in life.

Her sister Jazzmin, just two years older and often mistaken as Xana's twin, described their relationship as best friends who were always together. "She just was always fun," Jazzmin remembered. The sisters had an unbreakable bond that made Xana's loss even more devastating. Jazzmin was a senior at Washington State University, living only 15 minutes away, which meant the sisters saw each other regularly.

As a member of the Pi Beta Phi sorority alongside Maddie, Xana found her tribe among young women who shared her values and zest for life. She was the kind of person who made everyone around her feel special and included, which is why her loss rippled through so many lives.

Xana's relationship with Ethan Chapin showed her capacity for love and partnership. The couple had attended a Sigma Chi fraternity party together on their final night, enjoying the kind of normal college experience that should have led to years of memories together. Instead, they died together on the second floor of the house, where Xana had been awake when the killer entered, having just received a DoorDash order around 4 AM.

The family has honored Xana's memory by establishing a scholarship endowment, ensuring that her dream of changing lives continues even after her death. Her high school graduation cap message wasn't just teenage optimism – it was a prediction of the positive impact she would have had on the world.

Ethan Chapin: The Freshman Finding His Place

Ethan Chapin was just beginning to discover who he could become. At 20, this freshman from Conway, Washington, was one of triplets, part of a tight-knit family that included his siblings Maizie and Hunter. Coming to the University of Idaho represented his first real step into independence, and he was making the most of every opportunity.

What made Ethan special was his genuine kindness and the way he treated everyone with respect and warmth. As a member of the Sigma Chi fraternity, he was building the kinds of friendships that should have lasted a lifetime. His relationship with Xana Kernodle showed his capacity for love and commitment, even at his young age.

The night he died, Ethan had been staying over at the King Road house with Xana, something that had become routine in their relationship. They had enjoyed the Sigma Chi party together, returning to what they thought was the safety of home. Tragically, investigators believe Ethan was asleep when the killer struck, making him the last of the four victims to be targeted.

His parents' grief is captured in the simple fact that they were planning to celebrate not just one child's college experience, but three, with Ethan and his triplet siblings all navigating this crucial time together. The family's close bond made his loss all the more devastating.

The University of Idaho awarded Ethan a posthumous certificate in recreation, sport and tourism management, recognition of the path he was building toward a career that would have combined his interests with his natural ability to connect with others. His death robbed the world of someone who was just discovering his potential.

Bonds of Friendship: The Tight-Knit Group

The friendship between these four young people was the kind that defines college experiences and creates lifelong bonds. At the center of it all was the unbreakable connection between Maddie Mogen and Kaylee Goncalves, best friends since sixth grade who had grown up together in northern Idaho.

"They were sisters; she was one of ours," Kaylee's mother said about Maddie, capturing how their friendship had merged two families into one larger unit. Maddie's father Ben echoed this sentiment: "They were true sisters, and our families grew bigger and better from that." Their bond was so strong that they had followed each other through high school, chosen the same college, and eventually ended up as roommates sharing the adventure of college life.

Kaylee documented their friendship on social media, writing to Maddie on her 21st birthday: "I wouldn't have wanted anyone else to be the main character in all my childhood stories. I love you more than life! My best friend forever and more." It was a friendship that had weathered adolescence and was strong enough to last a lifetime.

Xana brought her own special energy to the group, connecting with Maddie through their work at Mad Greek restaurant and their shared membership in Pi Beta Phi sorority. Ethan completed the circle through his relationship with Xana, but he had also become friends with the other housemates in his own right.

The group's final social media post, taken just hours before the murders, shows all four victims together with two surviving roommates. Investigative journalist Howard Blum noted the eerie positioning: "On the ends of the picture are the two survivors... in the middle... are the victims... and they're huddled together." Kaylee's caption read: "one lucky girl to be surrounded by these ppl everyday 🖤" – words that now carry heartbreaking weight.

The three-story house at 1122 King Road should have been just another college rental, the kind of place where students create memories and learn independence. Instead, it became one of the most notorious crime scenes in recent American history. But before that terrible November night, it was simply home to six young women navigating college life together.

Maddie, Kaylee, and Xana shared the house with three other roommates, including Dylan Mortensen and Bethany Funke, who survived the attack. Former roommate Ashlin Couch, who had graduated in December 2021 and moved out in May 2022, remembered it as a place filled with friendship and laughter. She stayed in touch with Maddie and Kaylee, which made her text "Are you OK?" on the morning of November 13 even more poignant.

The house layout would prove crucial to understanding the tragedy. Kaylee's room on the third floor was small, with the bed taking up most of the space. Her parents described how someone entering the room would trap anyone inside: "You can't get out of that room. Completely, totally trapped. The bed was the entire room – could barely open up the door without swiping the foot of the bed."

For the young women who lived there, 1122 King Road represented freedom and friendship. They hosted gatherings, studied together, and built the kinds of relationships that should have lasted decades. Kaylee "loved living there with her friends" and "lived a happy life in that home," according to her mother.

The house became a symbol of everything that was lost that night. When the University of Idaho announced plans to demolish it, Kaylee's mother had mixed feelings: "I'm glad that somebody else isn't gonna live in it," but "my daughter lived in that home. She lived a happy life in that home." The decision to tear down the structure was described by university officials as "a healing step and removes the physical structure where the crime that shook our community was committed."

The demolition took place on December 28, 2023, exactly one year and 45 days after the murders. For Kristi Goncalves, watching on television as heavy equipment tore down her daughter's room was "horrible." But the house had become something beyond repair, "the grim reminder of the heinous act that took place there," as University President Scott Green explained.

These four young people – Maddie with her marketing dreams, Kaylee with her adventurous spirit, Xana with her entrepreneurial drive, and Ethan with his promising future – represent everything precious that was stolen on November 13, 2022. They weren't just victims in a crime; they were children, students, friends, and dreams cut short by inexplicable violence. Their stories remind us that behind every tragedy are real people with real lives, real futures, and real families who will never be the same.

Chapter 2: November 13, 2022 - The Final Hours

The Saturday that would become the most infamous night in Moscow, Idaho's history started like countless others in the college town. Students were making weekend plans, meeting friends, and heading out for another typical night of socializing. Four young people had no idea they were about to become part of a case that would grip the nation for months to come.

Saturday Night in Moscow: Different Paths, Same Destination

Moscow on November 12, 2022 was alive with the familiar energy of a Saturday night in a college town. The University of Idaho campus buzzed with students finishing up their weekend activities before what many expected to be their last normal weekend before Thanksgiving break. The weather was crisp but not bitterly cold, perfect for moving between indoor parties and outdoor gatherings.

Madison Mogen and Kaylee Goncalves had made plans to go downtown to their favorite hangout spot. These two were practically inseparable, best friends since sixth grade who had grown even closer during their senior year at the university. Madison, a 21-year-old marketing major from Coeur d'Alene, and Kaylee, also 21 and studying general studies from

Rathdrum, had that kind of friendship where they could communicate with just a look across a crowded room.

Meanwhile, Ethan Chapin and Xana Kernodle had their own Saturday night agenda. Ethan, a 20-year-old freshman from Conway, Washington, was still finding his rhythm in college life, but he'd found his anchor in Xana, a 20-year-old junior from Avondale, Arizona. The couple had become a familiar sight around campus, Ethan's quiet steadiness balancing perfectly with Xana's vibrant personality.

What none of them could have predicted was that their separate evening plans would converge in the most tragic way possible. Both groups were planning to end up back at the house on King Road where Madison, Kaylee, and Xana lived with two other roommates. It was a typical college arrangement in a town where off-campus housing was both affordable and close to campus.

The house at 1122 King Road had become a gathering place for their friend group. It was a three-story home with six bedrooms, two on each floor, nestled in a quiet residential area just steps from the university. The location made it perfect for college students who wanted to be close to campus but still have their own space away from dorm life.

Around 10:00 PM on November 12, Madison and Kaylee made their way to The Corner Club, a popular downtown sports bar that had become the unofficial heart of Greek life on campus. Located at 202 N. Main Street, the club was known for drawing capacity crowds on Friday and Saturday nights, filled with University of Idaho students looking to unwind after a week of classes.

The Corner Club wasn't just any bar to Madison and Kaylee. Both young women had connections to the service industry in Moscow. Madison and Xana both worked as servers at the Mad Greek restaurant, a local establishment where Bryan Kohberger had reportedly dined in the past, though this connection wouldn't become relevant until much later in the investigation.

Inside The Corner Club, surveillance cameras captured the two friends socializing with other patrons, laughing and enjoying what appeared to be a completely normal Saturday night out. A leaked surveillance image that later circulated on social media showed them around 1:32 AM, looking relaxed and happy as they mingled with the crowd. Madison Moye, a fellow student who saw Madison at the bar that night, later described the scene as totally ordinary. "It was just a normal night in Moscow," she told reporters. "Moscow is a safe place. Nothing like this ever happens."

The atmosphere in The Corner Club that night was typical for a Saturday in November. Students were celebrating the end of another week, some were already thinking ahead to Thanksgiving break, and others were just enjoying the company of friends. Madison and Kaylee fit right into this scene, two seniors who had become regulars at the establishment over their years at the university.

What made this night different wasn't anything that happened at The Corner Club itself. The bar provided exactly what Madison and Kaylee were looking for - a chance to relax, socialize, and enjoy each other's company. According to witnesses and surveillance footage, they stayed at the bar from approximately 10:00 PM until 1:30 AM, spending over three hours in what would be their final social gathering with a large group of friends.

The Corner Club's staff and management, like everyone else in Moscow, would later be devastated by what happened. The establishment posted a heartfelt message on Facebook the day after the murders: "Our hearts are hurting. Hug your loved ones, call that friend you haven't talked to for too long, be there for each other, travel home safely."

The Sigma Chi Party: Ethan and Xana's Evening Together

While Madison and Kaylee were downtown at The Corner Club, Ethan and Xana were attending a very different kind of gathering. They spent their evening at an on-campus party at the Sigma Chi fraternity house, an event that started around 8:00 PM and created the perfect college Saturday night atmosphere that Ethan was still getting used to as a freshman.

Ethan had actually started his evening at a formal event with his sister before meeting up with Xana at the Sigma Chi house. The fraternity party was the kind of gathering that typified weekend social life at the University of Idaho - music, conversation, and the comfortable camaraderie of students letting off steam after a week of academic pressures.

For Xana, these kinds of gatherings were familiar territory. As a junior, she had established herself as someone with a vibrant social presence on campus. She was known for her entrepreneurial spirit, having started a small business selling funnel cakes, and for her warm personality that drew people to her. Ethan, being newer to the college scene, was still finding his place, but with Xana by his side, he seemed to be settling into the rhythm of university life.

The Sigma Chi house party wasn't anything out of the ordinary for a Saturday night in November. Students moved between different social circles, some stayed for hours while others dropped by briefly before heading to other gatherings. It was the kind of fluid social environment where college relationships were built and maintained.

What investigators would later piece together was that Ethan and Xana stayed at the party until sometime between 8:00 and 9:00 PM, then returned home to the King Road house around 1:45 AM. This timing would prove crucial to understanding the timeline of that tragic night, though at the time, it was simply two young people ending their evening and heading back to what they expected to be the safety of home.

The fact that both couples - Madison and Kaylee from downtown, Ethan and Xana from the fraternity party - were converging on the same location around the same time would later seem like a cruel twist of fate. But on November 12, it was just the natural flow of a Saturday night in college town, where different social circles often ended up in the same places as the evening wound down.

At approximately 1:40 AM on November 13, Madison Mogen and Kaylee Goncalves appeared in what would become some of the most scrutinized footage in the entire investigation. After leaving The Corner Club around 1:30 AM, the two friends made their way to a late-night food truck in downtown Moscow, where they would be captured on a Twitch livestream that was broadcasting from the Grub Truckers food truck.

The Grub Truck, operated by Grub Wandering Kitchen, was stationed in Friendship Square and had become one of Moscow's few late-night dining options for hospital workers, students leaving bars, and anyone looking for food after most restaurants had closed. Joseph Woodall, the 26-year-old manager of the food truck, was running a live Twitch stream that night, a common practice that helped build community around the mobile eatery.

In the video, Madison and Kaylee can be seen approaching the truck with genuine smiles on their faces, looking completely relaxed and normal. They ordered $10 worth of carbonara and waited about 10 minutes for their food to be prepared. During this time, they chatted with each other and with other people standing near the truck, creating the kind of casual late-night social atmosphere that was typical for downtown Moscow on weekend nights.

31

What makes this footage so haunting in retrospect is how utterly ordinary everything appears. Madison and Kaylee show no signs of distress, fear, or awareness that anything unusual might be happening. They're just two college seniors grabbing some late-night food after a night out with friends. Joseph Woodall later told CNN that the two students "did not seem to be in distress or in danger in any way."

The video also captured other people in the area, including a man in a jacket and hoodie who was seen near Madison and Kaylee. This individual would later become a subject of intense speculation on social media, but police ultimately determined that he was not connected to the crime. Additional surveillance footage from the area showed the two women walking with this man and discussing someone named "Adam," but again, investigators found no connection to what would happen later that morning.

During their wait at the food truck, over a dozen other young people can be seen in the background, mostly chatting and joking as they waited for food. It was exactly the kind of late-night college scene that plays out in towns across America every weekend - young people extending their Saturday night just a little longer with friends and food.

The significance of this video to the investigation cannot be overstated. As Moscow Police Chief James Fry explained, the livestream provided investigators with "a time and space where two of our victims were." It established a crucial timeline and showed that Madison and Kaylee were behaving normally just hours before their deaths, ruling out several theories about what might have motivated the attack.

After getting their food, Madison and Kaylee were given a ride home by a private party. Police later determined that this driver was not involved in the crime and was simply providing a safe ride home for the two women.

Coming Home: The House on King Road After Midnight

The convergence at 1122 King Road happened almost simultaneously. Ethan and Xana arrived home around 1:45 AM after their evening at the Sigma Chi party, while Madison and Kaylee returned at approximately the same time after their food truck stop and rode home from downtown. The timing meant that all four future victims were in the house together by around 2:00 AM.

The house on King Road represented the kind of independence that college students crave. With six bedrooms spread across three floors, it provided privacy while still offering the community aspect that made college life social and fun. Madison and Xana lived there as regular tenants, while Kaylee had recently moved out but had returned that weekend to show Madison her new car and spend time with her best friend.

Dylan Mortensen and Bethany Funke, the two surviving roommates, were also in the house that night. They had been out in Moscow as well, enjoying their own Saturday night activities before returning home. By all accounts, the house settled into a typical early Sunday morning routine around 2:00 AM, with everyone back from their respective evening activities.

The layout of the house would prove crucial to understanding how the attack unfolded. Madison and Kaylee were on the third floor, where Kaylee was staying in Madison's room for the weekend. Xana and Ethan were on the second floor in Xana's bedroom. Dylan and Bethany were on the first floor, in what turned out to be the safest location in the house that night.

What happened in those first two hours after everyone came home remains largely a mystery. Text messages, phone calls, and social media activity suggest that the occupants of the house were winding down from their evening activities in the normal way college students do - probably talking about their nights, checking social media, and gradually settling in for sleep.

Kaylee had posted a photo earlier that day on Instagram showing the entire friend group together, with the caption "one lucky girl to be surrounded by these ppl everyday" followed by a heart emoji. It was a snapshot of the kind of tight-knit friendship group that makes college years so memorable, and it would become one of the last images of all four victims together.

The house that had been a sanctuary for friendship and college memories was about to become a crime scene that would haunt Moscow, Idaho forever.

The period between 2:00 AM and 4:00 AM on November 13, 2022 represents some of the most crucial and mysterious hours in the entire Idaho murders case. During this time, the four victims and two surviving roommates were all in the house, transitioning from the social energy of Saturday night to what should have been the quiet safety of home.

Based on digital evidence and witness statements that would later emerge, this appears to have been a period of normal nighttime activity. People were likely using their phones, possibly talking about their evenings, and gradually preparing for sleep. For college students, especially on a Saturday night stretching into Sunday morning, staying up until 2:00 or 3:00 AM wasn't unusual.

What investigators would later piece together from cell phone data, surveillance footage, and witness accounts is that this was when Bryan Kohberger's white Hyundai Elantra made multiple passes by the house. According to the probable cause affidavit released after his arrest, surveillance cameras captured a white or light-colored Elantra making several trips through the area beginning around 3:29 AM.

The car was seen passing by the victims' home three times before entering the area for a fourth time at 4:04 AM. This pattern of reconnaissance would later be interpreted by investigators as the perpetrator planning and timing his attack. At 4:20 AM, the same vehicle was captured speeding away from the neighborhood, which aligns with the timeframe investigators believe the murders occurred.

During these critical hours, Kohberger's cell phone went silent from 2:47 AM to 4:48 AM, a gap that investigators believe corresponds with the planning and execution of the attack. When the phone reconnected to the network, it was near Blaine, Idaho, which is along the route between Moscow and Pullman, Washington, where Kohberger was living as a PhD student.

Inside the house during this time, the surviving roommates would later tell investigators that they heard various sounds that they initially attributed to normal household activity or potentially partying. Dylan Mortensen reported hearing what she thought might be crying or playing around, sounds that weren't unusual in a house full of college students on a weekend night.

Around 4:00 AM, according to investigators, the killer entered the house. There was no sign of forced entry, which suggested either the door was unlocked or the perpetrator had some other means of access. The attack that followed was swift and brutal, with investigators believing it lasted only about 15 to 20 minutes.

At approximately 4:17 AM, a security camera less than 50 feet from Xana's room picked up the sound of a barking dog and what was described as "distorted audio of what sounded like voices or a whimper followed by a loud thud." This audio evidence would later become part of the prosecution's timeline of events.

The most chilling aspect of these silent hours is how quickly normal college life transitioned into unimaginable tragedy. In the span of less than two hours, four young people went from the safety and comfort of home to becoming victims of one of Idaho's most shocking crimes.

What makes this period even more haunting is that Dylan Mortensen, one of the surviving roommates, actually encountered the killer during his escape. She later told investigators that she opened her bedroom door after hearing sounds and saw a man "clad in black clothing and a mask" walking toward the house's sliding glass door. She described him as 5'10" or taller, not very muscular but athletically built, with bushy eyebrows.

The terror of that moment - seeing a masked stranger in her home in the early morning hours - caused Dylan to freeze in shock. She locked herself in her room and didn't call 911 until much later, a decision that would later generate controversy but which investigators understood as a trauma response.

By 4:25 AM, investigators believe the attack was over. Madison Mogen, Kaylee Goncalves, Xana Kernodle, and Ethan Chapin were dead, killed by what authorities determined was a large fixed-blade knife. The weapon was never found at the scene, but a tan leather knife sheath was left behind on Madison's bed, containing DNA that would eventually lead investigators to Bryan Kohberger.

The house fell silent after the attack, with the surviving roommates unaware of the tragedy that had occurred just floors above them. It wouldn't be until 11:58 AM on Sunday, November 13, that a 911 call would finally bring help to 1122 King Road, but by then, it was far too late for Madison, Kaylee, Xana, and Ethan.

Those silent hours between 2:00 and 4:00 AM would become the focus of one of the most intensive investigations in Idaho's history, as law enforcement worked to piece together exactly how four promising young lives were cut short in what should have been the safety of their own home.

Chapter 3: Horror in the Dark - The Murders Unfold

The clock on Dylan Mortensen's phone read 4:00 AM when the noises started. What she first dismissed as her roommate Kaylee playing with her dog upstairs would soon become the soundtrack to one of the most brutal crimes in Idaho's history. In just twenty-five minutes, four young lives would be extinguished in their sleep, a killer would vanish into the November darkness, and two surviving roommates would be left with memories that would haunt them forever.

The killer entered through the sliding glass door at the back of the house at approximately 4:00 AM. According to investigators, the homicides occurred between 4:00 and 4:25 AM, a twenty-five-minute window of terror that would forever change the quiet college town of Moscow, Idaho.

The house at 1122 King Road sat in darkness, its occupants settled into their bedrooms after a typical Saturday night out. Kohberger's phone had stopped connecting to the network around 2:47 AM in Pullman on November 13 before reconnecting around 4:48 AM near Blaine, Idaho, suggesting a deliberate effort to avoid digital tracking during the murders.

The three-story rental home had become familiar territory to the intruder. Kohberger's phone had pinged off cell towers near the home on at least twelve occasions prior to the killings, almost exclusively in the late evening and early-morning hours. He knew the layout, knew the routines, and knew exactly when the house would be most vulnerable.

Surveillance video showed the suspect's white Hyundai Elantra go by the victims' house three times, before entering the area for a fourth time at 4:04 AM. The methodical approach suggested careful planning and reconnaissance. This wasn't a crime of opportunity—it was a premeditated murder carried out with chilling precision.

The killer moved through the house like a shadow, armed with a large fixed-blade knife. A murder weapon was not found at the home, but the sheath of the knife was found in one of the bedrooms. The Ka-Bar style knife he carried was designed for military use, capable of inflicting devastating wounds with surgical efficiency.

Third Floor Terror: Madison and Kaylee's Final Moments

The attack began on the third floor, where best friends Madison Mogen and Kaylee Goncalves had their bedrooms. Goncalves and Mogen were both found in Goncalves' bedroom, as was the dog that Goncalves shared with her ex-boyfriend. The two young women, inseparable since sixth grade, would die together just as they had lived—side by side.

Mortensen heard what she thought sounded like Goncalves playing with her dog in one of the upstairs bedrooms, which were located on the third floor. These sounds, initially dismissed as normal nighttime activity, were likely the beginning of the attack. The killer had found his first victims asleep and vulnerable.

The forensic evidence painted a horrific picture. Authorities found one bedroom with a dog, where both Goncalves and Mogen were deceased with visible stab wounds. The violence was swift and brutal. An Idaho coroner revealed that their wounds were pretty extensive and the crime scene was unlike anything she'd experienced before.

Authorities later noticed a tan leather knife sheath laying next to Mogen's right side bearing the U.S. Marine Corps insignia and crucial DNA evidence on the button snap. This single piece of evidence—left behind either by accident or in the chaos of the attack—would ultimately seal the killer's fate. The sheath contained DNA that would be matched to Bryan Kohberger weeks later through genetic genealogy.

The two friends fought for their lives in those final moments. Evidence suggested they had tried to defend themselves and each other, but the surprise attack and the killer's weapon gave them little chance. Their bond, which had lasted through childhood and college, ended in the darkness of that November morning.

The killer then moved to the second floor, where Xana Kernodle and her boyfriend Ethan Chapin were spending the night together. Law enforcement determined Kernodle received a DoorDash order at approximately 4:00 AM and was still up using TikTok at approximately 4:12 AM. Unlike the victims on the third floor, Xana was awake when the killer reached her.

A short time later, Mortensen said she heard Goncalves say something to the effect of 'there's someone here,' though investigators pointed out that it could have been Kernodle's voice. The desperate warning echoed through the house—a final attempt to alert others to the danger that had invaded their home.

When Mortensen opened her door a second time, after hearing what she believed was crying coming from Kernodle's room, she heard a man's voice say something to the effect of 'It's OK, I'm going to help you'. These chilling words, spoken by the killer to his victim, demonstrated the calculated nature of his approach. He was calm, controlled, and methodical even in the midst of murder.

Inside the room, authorities found Chapin, who sustained deadly sharp-force injuries. Ethan, a freshman who was just beginning to find his place at the university, had tried to protect his girlfriend. The couple's final moments were spent together, facing an evil neither could have imagined.

Around 4:17 AM, a security camera less than 50 feet from Kernodle's bedroom wall picked up distorted audio of what sounded like voices, or a whimper followed by a loud thud. This audio evidence would later help investigators establish the precise timeline of the murders and confirm the narrow window during which the attacks occurred.

The Surviving Witnesses: Dylan and Bethany's Terrifying Night

Two roommates survived the massacre that night, saved by a combination of location, timing, and perhaps pure chance. The surviving roommates, Bethany Funke and Dylan Mortensen, slept in bedrooms on the first and second floors of the rental home. Their survival would provide crucial witness testimony that would help investigators identify and capture the killer.

Funke was staying in the basement of the house at the time of the murders and allegedly didn't witness the attack on her roommates. Her first-floor location may have saved her life, as the killer focused his attention on the upper floors where his intended victims were sleeping.

Panicked conversations between two surviving roommates were revealed in newly released text messages, shedding more light on the timeline that prosecutors aim to lean on in their case. The text exchanges between Dylan and Bethany painted a picture of confusion, fear, and growing horror as they realized something was terribly wrong.

Mortensen and Funke sent text messages to one another around 4:22 AM, with Mortensen writing 'I'm freaking out' to Funke. These messages, exchanged during the attacks, documented the terror experienced by the survivors in real-time. The timestamp showed that the killings were still in progress as the roommates tried to understand what was happening in their home.

Phone records show Mortensen tried calling the other four roommates but got no response around the time when a security camera from a residence close to the home picked up at 4:17 AM distorted audio of voices, a whimper, followed by a loud thud, and a barking dog. Her desperate attempts to reach her friends went unanswered because they were already dead or dying.

Dylan Mortensen's encounter with the killer represents one of the most chilling aspects of the entire case. Mortensen opened her door three times after waking up at around 4 AM, each time witnessing more evidence of the horror unfolding in her home.

She froze when she saw a figure clad in black clothing with a mask covering their mouth and nose walking toward her. The description she provided—a man, standing at either 5 feet 10 inches or taller, who was not very muscular, but athletically built with bushy eyebrows—would prove remarkably accurate when compared to Bryan Kohberger's physical appearance.

The roommate told police that the man walked past her while she stood at her bedroom doorway in a 'frozen shock phase,' and proceeded to exit the home through a sliding glass door at the back entrance. The psychological phenomenon Dylan experienced—becoming paralyzed by shock and fear—likely saved her life. Had she screamed or tried to run, she might have become the fifth victim.

Mortensen then tells Funke about seeing what looked like a man with a ski mask in the house, saying 'No it's like a ski mask almost'. Her immediate text to Bethany documented her terror in real-time, providing investigators with crucial contemporary evidence of the killer's appearance and behavior.

Dr. Akeem Marsh, a clinical professor of psychiatry, explained that it's possible Dylan went into a dissociation state and was just kind of confused and shocked and not really understanding what's going on. In those states, the mind is really shutting down to protect itself. This natural psychological response to extreme trauma helped explain why Dylan remained hidden and survived the encounter.

In his haste to escape or perhaps due to the adrenaline of the moment, the killer made a crucial mistake. Authorities later noticed a tan leather knife sheath laying next to Mogen's right side bearing the U.S. Marine Corps insignia and crucial DNA evidence on the button snap. This single piece of evidence would become the smoking gun that connected Bryan Kohberger to the crime scene.

The sheath wasn't just any piece of equipment—it was designed for a specific type of military-style knife. An Idaho coroner revealed the killer used a large knife, saying it would have had to have been not a pocket knife but a bigger knife. The Ka-Bar style weapon was designed for combat, capable of inflicting the kind of devastating wounds found on all four victims.

While processing the crime scene, detectives found a diamond-shaped footprint, potentially from a Vans sneaker, near Mortensen's bedroom door. This physical evidence placed the killer directly outside Dylan's room, confirming her account of seeing the masked figure walk past her door.

A DNA profile obtained from the trash from the Kohberger family residence matched the DNA profile obtained from the sheath, with at least 99.9998% of the male population expected to be excluded from the possibility of being the suspect's biological father. The genetic evidence was overwhelming—the odds that someone other than Bryan Kohberger left that DNA were virtually nonexistent.

The sheath would prove to be the killer's undoing. What he had planned as the perfect crime—no witnesses who could identify him, no surveillance footage of his face, no obvious connection to the victims—was undone by a single piece of leather bearing microscopic traces of his DNA. The evidence was so compelling that it would ultimately lead investigators across the country to a criminology student's family home in Pennsylvania, where they would make one of the most significant arrests in Idaho's criminal history.

The horror that unfolded in those twenty-five minutes at 1122 King Road would forever change not just the survivors and the families of the victims, but an entire community that had believed such evil couldn't touch their peaceful college town.

The evidence left behind would ensure that justice would eventually be served, but nothing could bring back the four young lives lost in the darkness of that November morning.

Chapter 4: The Making of a Suspect - Bryan Kohberger's Dark Journey

Bryan Christopher Kohberger was born in 1994 into a working-class family in Monroe County, Pennsylvania, nestled in the scenic Pocono Mountains. His father, Michael Kohberger Jr., worked as a maintenance worker for the Pleasant Valley School District, while his mother, Maryann, served as a paraprofessional supporting special-needs students in the same district. Bryan was the youngest of three children, with two older sisters, Amanda and Melissa.

The family faced financial struggles that would mark Bryan's early years. Court records reveal that his parents filed for bankruptcy twice—once in 1994, the year Bryan was born, and again when he was 14. During the second bankruptcy, they surrendered their house and car after facing $260,173 in debts with just $512 in the bank. Despite these hardships, both parents remained actively involved in the school system where Bryan would later attend.

Growing up in the gated Indian Mountain Lakes community in Albrightsville, Bryan was described by childhood neighbors as quiet and unremarkable. Natori Green, who lived just four doors down and graduated with Bryan in 2013, remembered him as part of the background rather than someone who stood out. The Pocono region itself struggled with significant drug problems, having one of the highest overdose death rates in Pennsylvania during the height of the opioid epidemic—a crisis that would later touch Bryan's own life.

His early childhood appeared relatively normal, with both parents working within the educational system that Bryan attended. Teachers and administrators recall no significant red flags during his elementary years, describing him as a regular student whose parents were notably involved in his education. However, those who knew him would later reflect that even then, Bryan seemed to be searching for something—validation, acceptance, or perhaps just a way to fit in.

Bryan's teenage years marked the beginning of concerning changes that would alarm those closest to him. During high school at Pleasant Valley, he was significantly overweight, weighing around 300 pounds, and became a frequent target of bullying. Former classmates remember him as an easy target who struggled socially and seemed increasingly isolated from his peers.

In his sophomore year, Bryan enrolled in the law enforcement program at Monroe County Technical Institute, where yearbook photos show him in uniform performing push ups during training. His stated goal was to become an Army Ranger, though his primary interest remained law enforcement. However, for reasons that remain unclear, he switched from the law enforcement track to HVAC studies in his junior year, following his father's career path.

The transformation began during his senior year when Bryan lost approximately 100 pounds through what friends describe as an obsessive approach to weight loss. Casey Arntz, whose brother was close to Bryan, recalled the dramatic change: "He was rail thin, and it was after that weight loss that a lot of people noticed a huge switch in him." This physical transformation came with behavioral changes that deeply concerned his friends.

Thomas Arntz, Bryan's close friend, experienced firsthand how Bryan's personality shifted after the weight loss. "When Bryan would get kinda angry with him, he would gaslight him and get physically aggressive," Casey Arntz later revealed. Bryan would put Thomas in headlocks and arm bars, behavior he tried to dismiss as "boys being boys" but which felt threatening and controlling to those on the receiving end.

During this period, Bryan also began associating with a different crowd—one involved with drugs. His pursuit of validation and acceptance led him down a dangerous path that would consume much of his late teenage years. For unclear reasons, Bryan transitioned to completing his senior year through online courses rather than attending in-person classes, raising questions about what might have prompted this change.

Academic Pursuits: From Community College to DeSales University

After graduating high school in 2013, Bryan's path forward was far from straight. His struggle with drug addiction intensified during the years immediately following graduation, with multiple friends confirming his battles with heroin use. One friend, referred to as Bree, watched Bryan's self-destructive spiral: "You just saw him becoming more self-destructive. He really stayed secluded."

The addiction reached a critical point in February 2014 when Bryan, recently out of rehab, stole his sister Melissa's iPhone and sold it at a mall kiosk for $200. His father reported the theft to police, leading to Bryan's arrest on misdemeanor charges. The case was later handled through Pennsylvania's Accelerated Rehabilitative Disposition program, allowing first-time offenders to have charges dropped and records expunged upon successful completion of probation.

Despite these setbacks, Bryan managed to get clean in 2016, marking a turning point in his life. Friends noticed the change, with Bree recalling his determination: "He was telling me that he wanted to get sober, that he was getting sober, and he wanted to let me know, 'I'm gonna do better.'" This period of sobriety coincided with Bryan's decision to pursue higher education seriously.

He enrolled at Northampton Community College, where he earned an associate degree in psychology in 2018. During this time, he also worked as a part-time security guard for the Pleasant Valley School District, the same system where his parents had worked. In one notable incident in 2018, Bryan was credited with helping save the life of a hall monitor who was having an asthma attack, demonstrating what appeared to be genuine concern for others.

His academic performance at community college was strong enough to gain admission to DeSales University in Center Valley, Pennsylvania, where he would pursue a bachelor's degree in psychology. This Catholic institution would become the setting for Bryan's deeper immersion into the study of criminal behavior and forensic psychology.

Bryan's time at DeSales University marked a period of intense personal reinvention that extended far beyond his earlier weight loss. Friends from this period, including Jack Baylis who had known him since eighth grade, noticed his continued fascination with psychology and human behavior. "He is super curious. Probably the most curious [person] who you'll ever meet," Baylis observed. "He was really into psychology, how people thought and whatnot."

The physical transformation that began in high school continued at DeSales. Bryan adopted veganism and maintained an extremely lean physique, though friends noted he required cosmetic surgery—a "tummy tuck"—to deal with excess skin from his dramatic weight loss. This attention to his physical appearance seemed part of a larger effort to remake himself entirely.

Academically, Bryan threw himself into his studies with an intensity that impressed his professors. Dr. Katherine Ramsland, a world-renowned forensic psychology professor famous for her interviews with serial killer Dennis Rader

(BTK), taught Bryan in several courses including "Psychology of Death Investigations." A former professor, Marie Bolger, later described Bryan as one of her brightest students, one of only two she had recommended for PhD programs in a decade.

However, classmates noticed troubling aspects of Bryan's personality during group projects and class discussions. One former classmate described him as "very intelligent" and "well spoken" but "seemingly detached." They recalled his "intense stare" and noted that "there wasn't much emotion displayed by him." Another student, Brittany Slaven, remembered Bryan's particular interest in serial killers, though at the time it seemed appropriate given their curriculum.

Bryan's academic work during this period would later prove chilling in retrospect. In May 2020, he wrote a 12-page paper entitled "Crime-scene Scenario Final" for a forensic investigation course. The assignment detailed a "crime toolkit" that should be used during crime scene investigation, including specific instructions about avoiding contamination through proper use of gloves and face masks to prevent leaving "hair, saliva, skin cells, and other bodily fluid."

Graduate School Ambitions: Why He Chose Criminal Justice

Upon completing his bachelor's degree in psychology in 2020, Bryan immediately continued his education at DeSales, pursuing a master's degree in criminal justice. His choice to focus on criminology seemed natural given his longstanding interest in law enforcement and psychology, but the intensity of his focus began to concern some who knew him.

During his graduate studies, Bryan conducted research that would later appear deeply troubling. In 2022, he posted a survey on Reddit seeking ex-convicts to participate in a DeSales research project that aimed to "understand how emotions and psychological traits influence decision-making when committing a crime." The survey asked detailed questions about criminal methodology, including how participants approached their victims, how they prepared for crimes, and whether they "struggled with or fought the victim."

Bryan's academic performance remained excellent, and he completed his master's degree in June 2022 with strong recommendations from faculty. His thesis work focused on criminal behavior analysis, and he demonstrated particular expertise in understanding crime scene dynamics and evidence handling. Professors saw him as a dedicated student with a bright future in criminal justice research.

However, those closer to him began noticing personality changes that suggested his academic interest in criminal behavior might be becoming something more personal. His social interactions became more strained, and he seemed increasingly focused on demonstrating his intellectual superiority over others. Friends noted that he "always wanted to be dominant physically and intellectually" and would argue aggressively with classmates, particularly women.

The completion of his master's degree marked another transition point for Bryan. Despite his academic success, those who knew him sensed that his interest in criminal behavior was evolving beyond scholarly curiosity into something that felt more visceral and personal.

In August 2022, Bryan moved across the country to begin his PhD in criminology and criminal justice at Washington State University in Pullman, Washington. The campus was just eight miles from Moscow, Idaho, and fifteen minutes from the house on King Road where he would allegedly commit the murders that would end four young lives.

At WSU, Bryan lived in graduate student housing and served as a teaching assistant while pursuing his doctoral studies. His initial impressions on fellow students were mixed. Benjamin Roberts, who took four classes with Bryan, remembered him as someone who "seemed comfortable around other people" and was "very quick to offer his opinion and thoughts." However, Roberts also noticed that Bryan appeared to be performing intelligence rather than simply being intelligent: "He would describe things in the most complicated, perhaps academic way possible. It was like he was trying to convince people that he knew what he was talking about."

Bryan's behavior in academic settings became increasingly problematic. An anonymous classmate recalled him frequently taking contrarian viewpoints and getting into heated arguments with other doctoral students, with his disagreements seeming to target women disproportionately. One incident led to a female doctoral student storming out of the classroom after accusing Bryan of "mansplaining."

As a teaching assistant, Bryan's conduct raised red flags among both faculty and students. Reports emerged of inappropriate behavior toward female students, with Bryan allegedly making them uncomfortable through personal questions and unwanted attention. Faculty received complaints about his "sexist attitude" and different treatment of male and female students. His behavior became serious enough that WSU initiated an investigation into his conduct.

In the months leading up to the Idaho murders, Bryan's behavior became increasingly erratic. Students in his classes noticed changes after November 12, 2022—the day of the murders. One student, Joey Famularo, recalled: "Definitely around then, he started grading everybody just 100s." Classmates observed that he became "a little more chatty" and "more animated" but also seemed perpetually exhausted, arriving late to classes with coffee in hand.

Bryan had also applied for an internship with the Pullman Police Department in 2022, expressing interest in "assisting rural law enforcement agencies with how to better collect and analyze technological data in public safety operations." His email to Police Chief Gary Jenkins after the interview showed his eagerness: "It was a great pleasure to meet with you today and share my thoughts and excitement regarding the research assistantship for public safety."

The irony was not lost on those who later learned of his arrest—a criminology PhD student studying the very crimes he allegedly committed, teaching future criminal justice professionals while potentially planning his own violent acts. Bryan's academic work had given him detailed knowledge of crime scene investigation, evidence handling, and law enforcement procedures—knowledge that would allegedly be put to use in the most horrific way possible.

On December 19, 2022, just weeks before his arrest, Bryan's teaching assistant position was terminated due to the ongoing investigation into his inappropriate conduct. Days later, he would drive across the country with his father, carrying with him the secrets of what investigators believe were his final moments as a free man before becoming the most wanted fugitive in America.

The transformation from a struggling, overweight teenager in Pennsylvania to a PhD student studying criminal behavior had taken nearly a decade. But somewhere along that journey, Bryan Kohberger had allegedly crossed a line from studying violence to perpetrating it, turning his academic knowledge into a blueprint for the murders that would shock the nation and forever change the lives of four families who lost their children to an unimaginable act of evil.

Chapter 5: Red Flags and Warning Signs

By fall 2022, Bryan Kohberger's carefully constructed academic facade was beginning to crack. What emerged from those fractures would reveal a disturbing pattern of behavior that, in retrospect, painted a chilling portrait of a man spiraling toward violence. The red flags were there, scattered across his digital footprint, witnessed in his interactions with female students, and documented in his increasingly erratic conduct at Washington State University. Yet like pieces of a puzzle no one knew they were assembling, these warning signs remained disconnected until it was too late.

The complaints began quietly in November 2022, just weeks before the murders. Female students in Kohberger's criminology classes started approaching faculty members with concerns about their teaching assistant's behavior. What they described was a pattern of conduct that made them deeply uncomfortable and fearful.

According to sources who worked with Kohberger at WSU, he allegedly told female colleagues that men were going to take their jobs because women aren't as smart. This wasn't casual sexism but something more calculated and cruel. Students complained that he talked down to female students and graded them unfairly compared to men during his time as a teaching assistant. The discrimination was so obvious that multiple students noticed the pattern independently.

But the inappropriate behavior went beyond grading disparities. One female student accused Kohberger of following her to her car, a violation that crossed the line from academic misconduct into potential stalking. Other women described feeling uncomfortable around him, reporting that he stared at them on campus in ways that felt predatory rather than academic.

The university investigated these allegations but found no evidence of wrongdoing, a decision that would later feel tragically inadequate. However, the pattern of complaints was serious enough that WSU held a harassment training seminar in the wake of those complaints, suggesting the administration recognized a problem even if they couldn't legally act on it.

What made these reports particularly disturbing was their timing. The complaints came in November 2022, just weeks before the Idaho murders. In his termination letter, officials allegedly noted that Kohberger had a "sexist attitude" toward the females that he interacted with at the school. The university was aware of his problematic behavior with women at the exact time he was allegedly planning his attack on female victims.

The Reddit Posts: Anonymous Confessions and Dark Thoughts

Seven months before the murders, Kohberger had posted something on Reddit that would later seem prophetic in its darkness. Using the handle "Criminology_Student," he posted a research survey asking people about their thoughts and feelings on their criminal activity. On the surface, it appeared to be legitimate academic research. Beneath that veneer lay something far more sinister.

The post read: "My name is Bryan, and I am inviting you to participate in a research project that seeks to understand how emotions and psychological traits influence decision-making when committing a crime. In particular, this study seeks to understand the story behind your most recent criminal offense, with an emphasis on your thoughts and feelings throughout your experience".

The questions within the survey revealed a mind obsessed with the mechanics of violence. Respondents were asked about their plans surrounding the idea of committing a crime: "Before making your move, how did you approach the victim or target? After committing the crime, what were you thinking and feeling?" The survey also asked: "Did you prepare for the crime before leaving your home?"

These weren't typical academic questions. They read like a playbook for someone planning their own criminal act. The survey was posted to a subreddit on ex-cons, suggesting Kohberger was specifically targeting people with experience in violent crime. The account has been suspended by Reddit and the posts removed, but screenshots preserved the chilling evidence of his preoccupation with criminal psychology.

What's particularly disturbing is how the survey questions mirror the alleged planning and execution of the Idaho murders. The emphasis on approaching victims, the focus on thoughts and feelings during the crime, and the questions about preparation all align with what prosecutors allege Kohberger did in Moscow. It's as if he was conducting research for his own future crimes.

The most damning evidence of Kohberger's premeditation came from his cell phone data, which revealed a pattern of behavior that can only be described as stalking. Investigators found that Kohberger's phone had pinged cell towers in the "coverage area" of the King Road home at least 12 times before the November murders.

These visits began as early as August 21, 2022, the day before his classes as a graduate student were set to begin at Washington State. All of his prior visits, except for one, were in the late evening or early morning, suggesting he was deliberately timing his surveillance to avoid detection.

The pattern revealed by cell phone experts shows something far more sinister than casual drives. According to FBI cell phone expert analysis obtained by "Dateline," Kohberger's phone connected to a cell tower providing coverage within 100 meters of the rental house at 1122 King Road. It connected 23 visits over four months, all after dark.

After attending a pool party in Moscow on July 9, Kohberger's phone data suggests he was in Moscow again that day after dark. Over the next month, his phone data indicates a dozen trips to Moscow, with his phone connecting to cell towers near the victims' home. This wasn't random driving or stargazing, as his defense would later claim. This was systematic surveillance of his future victims.

The frequency and timing of these visits paint a picture of escalating obsession. Between 10:34 and 11:35 pm on August 21, 2022, Bryan Kohberger's cell phone was detected as being close to the murder residence. Each visit brought him closer to the moment when surveillance would turn to violence.

Perhaps most chilling is what happened on the morning of the murders. Cell phone data shows that Kohberger returned to the scene of the crime at 9 am on November 13, just hours after the killings and about three hours before police received the 911 call. This return visit suggests he wanted to observe the aftermath of his work, a behavior consistent with serial killer psychology.

Digital Footprints: Online Searches and Amazon Purchases

Kohberger's digital behavior in the months leading up to the murders revealed a mind increasingly consumed with violence and sexual deviance. In late September, records from the criminology student's phone included an internet search for "Sociopathic Traits in College Student," and the following month, there was a search for pornography containing keywords "drugged" and "sleeping".

These searches weren't academic research. They reflected personal interests that aligned disturbingly with the nature of his alleged crimes. The victims were attacked while sleeping, and the search for content involving "drugged" and "sleeping" individuals suggests he was fantasizing about attacking helpless victims.

Even more damning were Kohberger's Amazon purchases. Prosecutors allege that Kohberger had purchased a Ka-Bar knife, sheath, and sharpener on Amazon eight months before the murders. This wasn't an impulse purchase but part of a long-term plan. The fact that he bought a sheath along with the knife suggests he understood the need to carry the weapon concealed.

After the murders, his search history showed more videos of Ted Bundy, the song "Criminal" by Britney Spears and additional selfies, including Kohberger wearing a black hoodie like how Bundy was dressed in a program viewed on YouTube. This post-murder behavior suggests he was comparing himself to famous serial killers and possibly planning additional attacks.

The digital evidence reveals a man who was methodically preparing for violence while simultaneously studying it academically. His online behavior showed an escalating obsession with criminal psychology, violent content, and non-consensual sexual material that created a perfect storm of dangerous fixations.

By December 2022, Kohberger's professional facade was completely collapsing. The termination letter from WSU was dated December 19, 2022, more than a month after the killings of Kaylee Goncalves, Madison Mogen, Ethan Chapin and Xana Kernodle on November 13. However, the problems that led to his firing had been building for months.

The letter referenced a September 23, 2022 "altercation" between Kohberger and Professor John Snyder, whom he was assisting as a teaching assistant. On October 21, Professor Snyder emailed Kohberger about "the ways in which you had failed to meet your expectations as a TA thus far in the semester".

Kohberger was put on an improvement plan on November 2, just 11 days before the four Idaho students were found stabbed to death in their off-campus home. The timing is significant. He was facing professional failure and academic humiliation at the exact moment prosecutors allege he was finalizing his plans for murder.

A second argument with the same teacher on December 9 motivated the university to fire him for not making "progress regarding professionalism". The decision to eliminate his funding and terminate his role was reportedly based on his unsatisfactory performance as a teaching assistant and his failure to meet the "norms of professional behavior".

Former FBI agent Jennifer Coffindaffer noted that the details outlined in the termination letter indicate that Kohberger had known something "could be going awry with his position" in the months leading up to November 13. The mounting professional pressure may have been a catalyst that pushed him toward violence.

The investigation into his conduct around female students was discussed during an end-of-year meeting among WSU's criminology department, showing that faculty were aware of serious problems with their teaching assistant. Yet somehow, he remained in his position long enough to allegedly commit quadruple murder.

In the final weeks before the murders, Kohberger's behavior became increasingly erratic and suspicious. The convergence of his academic failure, investigation for misconduct, and escalating surveillance of the King Road house created the perfect conditions for his alleged explosion into violence.

Multiple complaints had been made to the university regarding his conduct with both female colleagues and students. The pressure was mounting from all directions. His academic career was crumbling, his behavior toward women was under investigation, and his carefully maintained facade of normalcy was disintegrating.

The cell phone data shows that his surveillance of the victims intensified in the days immediately before the attack. Ten days after he moved to Pullman in June 2022, he was invited to a pool party in Moscow, where attendees told "Dateline" they had awkward interactions with Kohberger. This may have been when he first became aware of the King Road house and its occupants.

A former female graduate student said Kohberger put his number in her phone and texted her the next day mentioning how they had chatted about hiking. The text read in part: "I really enjoy that activity so please let me know." The woman noted: "The wording of the text, as I look back on it, is kind of peculiar".

This interaction reveals Kohberger's pattern of inappropriate contact with women and his skill at making seemingly innocent overtures that left recipients feeling uncomfortable. It also shows he was actively networking within the Moscow social scene, possibly gathering intelligence about potential victims.

By November 2022, all the warning signs had converged. His professional life was in ruins, his behavior toward women had been reported to authorities, his digital footprint revealed violent obsessions, and his physical surveillance of the victims had reached a crescendo. The red flags were everywhere, but they remained scattered across different institutions and individuals who had no way of seeing the complete picture.

The tragedy of these warning signs is not just that they existed, but that they were never connected in time to prevent the violence that followed. Kohberger had been studied, investigated, disciplined, and fired, yet he remained free to complete his alleged plan. The system designed to identify and stop dangerous individuals had all the pieces but failed to assemble them into action.

In retrospect, the path from warning signs to violence seems inevitable. Each red flag represents a missed opportunity to intervene, a chance to prevent four young lives from being lost to one man's descent into darkness. The signs were there, waiting for someone to connect them into the horrifying truth of what Bryan Kohberger was planning to become.

Chapter 6: Seven Weeks of Terror - The Investigation Begins

The horror began to unfold at 11:58 a.m. on November 13, 2022, when a chilling 911 call shattered the quiet Sunday morning in Moscow, Idaho. The frantic voice on the other end of the line would deliver news that would transform this peaceful college town forever.

"Something has happened in our house, and we don't know what," a crying woman told the dispatcher, her voice trembling with fear and confusion. The call, made from one of the surviving roommate's phones, initially seemed like a routine emergency involving an unconscious person. But the details that emerged painted a picture of something far more sinister.

"One of the roommates passed out. And she was drunk last night and she's not waking up," another woman explained, taking the phone. The callers believed their friend Xana Kernodle had simply had too much to drink the night before and wouldn't respond to their attempts to wake her.

Then came the haunting detail that would send chills through the community: "Oh, and they saw some man in their house last night."

The surviving roommates, Dylan Mortensen and Bethany Funke, had woken up that morning with fragments of a terrifying night. Between 4:19 a.m. and 4:32 a.m., they had tried calling and texting their housemates multiple times. Madison and Kaylee never answered. Neither did Xana. The silence should have been their first warning.

Hours passed before they finally called friends over to the house because they thought one of the victims on the second floor had passed out and wasn't waking up. When police arrived at 1122 King Road, they found the door to the residence open. There was no sign of forced entry, no damage inside the house, and nothing appeared to be missing. But what they discovered inside would haunt the small police force for months to come.

All four students were pronounced dead at noon. The scene was so traumatic that Latah County Coroner Cathy Mabbutt later told reporters, "It was a pretty traumatic scene to find four dead college students in a residence." The victims had been stabbed multiple times with what police believed was a large fixed-blade knife. Some had defensive wounds, suggesting they had fought for their lives.

Crime Scene Chaos: Securing Evidence at 1122 King Road

The three-story rental house on King Road became the center of one of the most complex crime scenes Idaho investigators had ever encountered. For a small police department that hadn't handled a murder since 2015, the quadruple homicide presented unprecedented challenges.

The layout of the house complicated everything. Madison Mogen and Kaylee Goncalves were found dead in Mogen's third-floor bedroom, sharing the same bed where they had died together. One floor below, Xana Kernodle and her boyfriend Ethan Chapin were discovered in Kernodle's second-floor bedroom. The two surviving roommates had been sleeping on the first floor and somehow escaped the killer's notice.

Police found Kaylee's dog, Murphy, alive and unharmed on the third floor. The fact that the dog hadn't alerted the household to an intruder raised immediate questions about how the killer had moved through the house so silently and efficiently.

The crime scene yielded crucial evidence that would prove pivotal weeks later. A tan leather Ka-Bar knife sheath was found on the bed next to Madison Mogen's body. This single piece of evidence contained DNA that would eventually lead investigators to their suspect, though they didn't know it yet.

The house had been a party location where friends routinely came and went, which meant DNA from dozens of people could be found throughout the residence. Howard Ryan, a former commander of a crime scene unit in the New Jersey State Police, explained the complexity: "Murder investigations are not a spectator event. People are influenced by TV shows. They believe that these events and processing and work happens at a much more rapid pace and results are obtained much quicker than they really are."

The investigation team faced the monumental task of collecting and processing hundreds of DNA samples, then looking for a potential suspect's genetic profile among them. Blood evidence was everywhere, but investigators had to determine which belonged to victims and which might belong to the perpetrator.

Processing the digital evidence proved equally challenging. Cell phone records, surveillance footage from nearby cameras, and social media activity all had to be analyzed. The Moscow Police Department, with limited resources for such a complex case, immediately called in the Idaho State Police and FBI for assistance.

The investigation's early days were marked by confusion, miscommunication, and several critical missteps that experts would later criticize. For a small police force unaccustomed to major crimes, the intense public scrutiny and media attention created additional pressure to provide answers they simply didn't have.

Moscow Police Chief James Fry made his first major misstep three days after the murders when he assured the community that there was "no imminent threat to the public." This premature statement would later be walked back, but the damage was done. Retired NYPD Sergeant Joseph Giacalone called it a significant error: "They don't have an identified suspect, and they still don't have a motive, so until you have those two extremely vital pieces you can't set the public's mind at ease."

The confusion deepened when Moscow Mayor Art Bettge, who had no background in criminology, told the New York Times that the attack was a "crime of passion." He later backpedaled, but his comments had already fueled speculation and theories that would prove completely wrong.

Latah County Coroner Cathy Mabbutt created another controversy by sharing specific details about the autopsies during television interviews. She revealed that victims were stabbed multiple times in the torso, ambushed in their sleep, and some had defensive wounds. She called the attack "personal." Criminal justice experts were appalled by these revelations. "It was not only surprising but aggravating," Giacalone said of the coroner's media appearances.

Police initially described the killings as a "targeted attack," suggesting the victims or house had been specifically chosen. This led to extensive investigation into the victims' personal lives, relationships, and potential conflicts. However, investigators later admitted they weren't certain whether the residence or any occupants were specifically targeted, calling their earlier statement a "miscommunication."

Early theories focused on possible stalkers, especially regarding Kaylee Goncalves. Police investigated reports that she had been followed in a local business in mid-October, but these leads proved fruitless. They also examined the victims' relationships, including Kaylee's ex-boyfriend and other potential romantic connections.

The investigation initially pursued several wrong directions. Police spent considerable time examining a man captured in surveillance footage near a food truck where Madison and Kaylee had been hours before the murders. The hooded figure sparked intense speculation, but police later confirmed he had no connection to the crime.

Community in Crisis: Fear Grips the University of Idaho

The murders sent shockwaves through Moscow's tight-knit community of 25,000 residents. The University of Idaho, which hadn't experienced such violence in recent memory, found itself at the center of a national media storm. Students and parents demanded answers, security, and assurance that it was safe to remain on campus.

Classes were canceled on November 14, the day after the murders. The university scheduled a candlelight vigil for November 16, then postponed it as the investigation intensified. Students began leaving campus in droves, many driven home by worried parents who refused to let their children stay in what felt like a war zone.

The psychological impact on the community was devastating. Hardware stores reported selling out of security devices "faster than toilet paper during the pandemic." Students who remained on campus traveled in groups, avoided going out after dark, and many slept with weapons nearby.

Local businesses suffered as the once-vibrant college town atmosphere evaporated. Restaurants and bars that typically bustled with student activity found themselves nearly empty. The economic impact rippled through the community as fear replaced the normal rhythms of college life.

The surviving roommates faced particularly intense scrutiny and speculation. Online conspiracy theorists questioned their actions, their timeline, and even their potential involvement. Police repeatedly stated that Dylan Mortensen and Bethany Funke were not suspects, but the public's hunger for answers led to relentless examination of their every move.

Parents across the country questioned whether their own college-aged children were safe. The case struck a particular nerve because it shattered the assumption that students living off-campus in a small college town were relatively protected from such extreme violence.

University of Idaho President Scott Green found himself managing a crisis that threatened the institution's very survival. Enrollment concerns, safety protocols, and media management became daily challenges as the campus struggled to maintain some semblance of normalcy while a killer remained at large.

After weeks of following dead ends and processing thousands of tips, investigators finally caught their first significant break. On December 7, nearly four weeks after the murders, Moscow Police made a public appeal that would prove pivotal: they were looking for information about a white 2011-2013 Hyundai Elantra seen in the immediate area of the victims' house during the early morning hours of November 13.

The announcement electrified the investigation and the public's attention. Police had identified this vehicle through painstaking analysis of surveillance footage from cameras in the area. The car had been captured making multiple passes near the residence around the time of the murders, a pattern that immediately raised suspicions.

Surveillance recordings showed the white Elantra passing by the victims' home three times, beginning around 3:29 a.m. At 4:04 a.m., the vehicle returned for a fourth time. Then, at 4:20 a.m., cameras captured it speeding away from the victims' neighborhood. The timing aligned perfectly with the window investigators believed the murders had occurred.

The public response was immediate and overwhelming. Tips poured in from across the country as people reported white Elantras in their neighborhoods, parking lots, and driveways. Police announced they were searching records of approximately 22,000 fifth-generation Hyundai Elantras made between 2011 and 2013.

What the public didn't know yet was that investigators in neighboring Pullman, Washington, had already begun focusing on one particular white Elantra. The car belonged to a 28-year-old PhD candidate and teaching assistant named Bryan Christopher Kohberger, who lived just eight miles from the murder scene.

Kohberger's vehicle had come to their attention through routine police work. Washington State University campus police had documented his car during a traffic stop in October 2022, about a month before the killings. He had been pulled over for allegedly running a red light in Pullman and was let go with a warning.

The Elantra announcement represented a masterful piece of police strategy. Rather than immediately arresting Kohberger and potentially alerting him to their investigation, they used the public appeal to gather additional information while building their case. They were already conducting surveillance on Kohberger and gathering evidence, but they needed time to solidify their forensic findings.

Social Media Frenzy: Amateur Sleuths and False Accusations

The Idaho murders case coincided with the peak of true crime's popularity on social media, creating a perfect storm of public fascination and amateur investigation. What began as genuine concern for justice quickly devolved into a feeding frenzy of speculation, false accusations, and conspiracy theories that would devastate innocent lives.

TikTok, Facebook, and YouTube became hunting grounds for amateur detectives convinced they could solve the case faster than law enforcement. The hashtag #IdahoMurderMystery accumulated more than 207 million views on TikTok alone. Facebook groups dedicated to the case attracted hundreds of thousands of members, with the largest reaching over 227,000 participants.

The consequences were devastating for several innocent individuals who found themselves falsely accused. Rebecca Scofield, a University of Idaho professor, became a target after an online tarot card reader claimed to have divined her guilt through supernatural means. The baseless accusations spread across social media platforms, upending Scofield's life and forcing her to file a defamation lawsuit.

Brent Kopacka, a 36-year-old Purple Heart recipient who died in an unrelated police shooting in December 2022, was posthumously accused of the Idaho murders by online conspiracy theorists. Scores of posts on TikTok, Facebook, and YouTube tied his name to the crime, devastating his family and friends who were already grieving his loss.

The food truck worker who had served Madison and Kaylee hours before their deaths faced relentless online harassment. Despite police statements that he was not involved, amateur sleuths dissected his every movement in the surveillance footage, creating elaborate theories about his potential guilt.

Moscow Police Captain Roger Lanier publicly addressed the problem, stating that "rumors and speculation has led members of the public to provide tips based on rumors rather than official information provided about the case." The department found itself overwhelmed not just with the investigation but with managing the misinformation spreading across social media platforms.

Some amateur sleuths did attempt to provide legitimate assistance. True crime enthusiasts created detailed timelines, mapped the victims' movements, and analyzed public information in ways that occasionally provided useful insights. However, the harmful speculation far outweighed any potential benefits.

The case highlighted the dark side of true crime's popularity. Online personalities built followings by promoting unsubstantiated theories, often generating income through monetized content that exploited the victims' deaths and destroyed innocent lives. The phenomenon became so problematic that Moscow Police issued multiple public warnings about the dangers of online speculation.

The social media frenzy also complicated the investigation itself. Detectives had to sort through thousands of tips based on internet rumors rather than factual observations. Resources that should have been focused on solving the case were diverted to managing public relations and debunking false theories.

As the seven weeks of terror continued, the combination of genuine investigative work and destructive online speculation created a unique challenge for law enforcement. The case would eventually be solved through traditional police work and modern forensic science, but not before social media's influence had left its own trail of damaged lives and compromised investigations.

The community's desperation for answers, combined with the unprecedented reach of social media platforms, had created a new kind of victim in true crime cases: the falsely accused innocent bystander whose life could be destroyed by viral speculation. It was a phenomenon that would force a reckoning with how modern society consumes and participates in real-time criminal investigations.

Chapter 7: The Hunt for Justice - Modern Forensics Crack the Case

The breakthrough that would change everything came from what appeared to be the killer's only mistake. On November 13, 2022, as Moscow Police Corporal Brett Payne walked through the blood-soaked crime scene at 1122 King Road, he noticed something that didn't belong. Next to Madison Mogen's body, partially hidden under her comforter, lay a tan leather knife sheath stamped with the U.S. Marine Corps eagle, globe, and anchor emblem. The killer had left behind what forensic experts would later call the "smoking gun" of the case.

The Idaho State Lab discovered a single source of male DNA on the button snap of the knife sheath. This wasn't just any DNA sample—it was what forensic experts call "touch DNA," the microscopic skin cells that transfer when someone handles an object. Rylene Nowlin, an Idaho State Police forensic laboratory manager, explained that these skin cells can be shed during normal handling and provide a genetic fingerprint as unique as the person who left it.

The significance of this evidence cannot be overstated. In a crime scene where the perpetrator appeared to have been methodical and careful, this single piece of evidence would prove to be his undoing. The DNA profile would later be determined to be at least 5.37 octillion times more likely to belong to Bryan Kohberger than to any unrelated individual randomly selected from the general population. To put this astronomical number in perspective, an octillion is a 1 followed by 27 zeros—a statistical certainty that bordered on the impossible to refute.

What made this evidence even more compelling was its location. The sheath wasn't randomly dropped or accidentally left behind—it was found on the bed where two of the victims lay murdered. This suggested the killer had either brought the sheath with him and lost it during the attack, or had removed the knife from its sheath at the scene. Either scenario pointed to this being evidence directly connected to the murders, not some random contamination or plant.

The forensic team handling this evidence knew they had something extraordinary. Unlike many criminal cases where DNA might be degraded, mixed with other samples, or too small to analyze properly, this sample was clean, substantial, and uncontaminated. It would become the cornerstone of the entire prosecution case against Bryan Kohberger.

Genetic Genealogy: Revolutionary Science Identifies a Suspect

With a clean DNA sample in hand, investigators faced a familiar challenge in modern criminal justice: the DNA didn't match anyone in the FBI's Combined DNA Index System (CODIS), the national database of criminal offenders. In previous decades, this might have meant the end of the DNA lead. But in 2022, law enforcement had a powerful new tool at their disposal—investigative genetic genealogy (IGG).

The FBI loaded the DNA profile from the knife sheath onto publicly available genealogy sites and began building family trees of genetic relatives to identify the contributor of the unknown DNA. This revolutionary technique, which had already solved cold cases like the Golden State Killer, was about to be used in one of the most high-profile active investigations in recent memory.

The process was both technologically sophisticated and deeply methodical. FBI genealogists constructed detailed family trees containing hundreds of individuals, mapping out bloodlines, birth dates, death dates, and familial connections stretching back generations. The product of the genealogy conducted by the FBI was a family tree that contained the name, birthdate, and death date (if applicable) of hundreds of relatives as well as their familial connections between each other and the suspect.

What emerged from this genetic detective work was extraordinary. Unlike traditional forensic approaches that might take months or years to identify a suspect, genetic genealogy was providing investigative leads in a matter of weeks. The technique works by comparing the crime scene DNA to massive databases of genetic information voluntarily submitted by people researching their ancestry, then using sophisticated algorithms to identify potential family relationships.

The FBI's genealogy work eventually produced a tip that pointed law enforcement toward Kohberger, though this tip alone didn't provide substantive evidence of guilt. But it gave investigators something invaluable: a name to investigate. This represented a paradigm shift in criminal investigation—instead of starting with suspects and working toward evidence, investigators could now start with evidence and work toward suspects.

The ethical implications of this technique sparked significant debate in the forensic community. Some argued that people who submitted DNA for ancestry research never consented to having their genetic information used in criminal investigations. Others countered that the technique only identified potential suspects who still needed to be investigated through traditional means. Regardless of the ethical debates, the technology was proving remarkably effective at solving previously unsolvable cases.

While genetic genealogy provided the suspect's name, investigators needed more than DNA to build a prosecutable case. They turned to the digital footprints that have become ubiquitous in modern life—cell phone data and surveillance footage that would paint a detailed picture of Bryan Kohberger's movements leading up to and during the murders.

Kohberger's AT&T cell phone, ending in the digits 8458, had pinged towers covering the King Road area at least 12 times between June and November 2022, mostly during late evening hours. This pattern of visits was particularly significant because it suggested reconnaissance behavior—someone repeatedly visiting an area during times when residents would likely be asleep or less vigilant.

The cell phone data from the night of the murders told an even more compelling story. At 2:42 AM on November 13, Kohberger's phone pinged a cell tower near his residence in Pullman, Washington. Then at 2:47 AM, his phone pinged again, showing movement south through Pullman. What happened next was perhaps the most incriminating digital evidence of all: his phone went completely silent.

Kohberger's phone stopped connecting to the cell network from 2:47 AM to 4:48 AM—precisely covering the timeframe when the murders occurred. When cell phones suddenly stop communicating with towers, it typically means one of three things: the phone is turned off, placed in airplane mode, or moved to an area without service. Given that Kohberger was traveling through populated areas of Idaho and Washington, the lack of service seemed unlikely.

Surveillance footage provided crucial corroboration for the cell phone evidence. Security cameras from Washington State University campus showed a white sedan matching Kohberger's vehicle heading toward Moscow around 3 AM and returning around 5:30 AM. Multiple cameras throughout the region captured what appeared to be the same white Hyundai Elantra traveling on routes that would connect Pullman to Moscow during the crucial time window.

When investigators later obtained a search warrant for Washington State University vehicle records, they discovered that Bryan Kohberger owned a 2015 white Hyundai Elantra, originally with Pennsylvania plates that had been registered in Washington. This vehicle matched the description of the car that Moscow police had been seeking since shortly after the murders.

The digital evidence extended beyond just location data. Investigators discovered that Kohberger had been stopped by police in August 2022 during a routine traffic stop, at which time he had provided his phone number to Moscow police. This seemingly innocent interaction would later provide investigators with the exact phone number they needed to subpoena his cellular records.

Building the Case: Connecting the Evidence to Bryan Kohberger

As investigators compiled their evidence throughout December 2022, a compelling circumstantial case began to emerge. The genetic genealogy had provided the suspect's identity, the DNA evidence linked him directly to the crime scene, and digital forensics placed him in the right location at the right time. But prosecutors needed more than individual pieces of evidence—they needed to weave them together into a narrative that would convince a judge there was probable cause for arrest.

The investigation revealed troubling patterns in Kohberger's behavior that went far beyond the night of the murders. His academic background as a criminology PhD student created an unsettling irony—here was someone studying the very techniques that would ultimately be used to capture him. His research interests in criminal behavior and his knowledge of forensic techniques raised questions about whether his academic pursuits had influenced his approach to committing crimes.

When investigators conducted their final analysis comparing Kohberger's cheek swab to the knife sheath DNA, the results were overwhelming—the STR profile was at least 5.37 octillion times more likely to be seen if Kohberger was the source than if an unrelated individual was the source. This statistical match was so astronomically high that it effectively eliminated any reasonable doubt about the DNA's origin.

The timing of everything was also significant. Kohberger had completed his semester at Washington State University and was preparing to leave for Pennsylvania for winter break. If investigators had waited much longer, their suspect would have been 2,500 miles away, potentially complicating extradition and arrest procedures. The pressure to move quickly was immense, but investigators had to balance urgency with the need for airtight probable cause.

The geographical aspects of the case also supported the prosecution's theory. Kohberger lived just nine miles from the murder scene, making the drive between Pullman and Moscow a routine trip that wouldn't raise suspicions. His familiarity with the area, combined with his multiple previous visits to the vicinity of the victims' home, suggested a level of planning and preparation that went far beyond a random crime of opportunity.

Perhaps most importantly, investigators found no evidence of any legitimate reason for Kohberger to have been in the King Road area during the early morning hours of November 13. He wasn't a student at the University of Idaho, didn't work in Moscow, and had no known connections to the victims or their social circles. His presence in the area during the murders, combined with his DNA at the crime scene, created a circumstantial case that prosecutors believed was strong enough to obtain an arrest warrant.

Once investigators had identified Bryan Kohberger as their primary suspect, they faced a logistical challenge: he was no longer in Idaho. In mid-December 2022, Kohberger had driven cross-country to Pennsylvania to spend winter break with his family. What appeared to be a routine holiday trip would become one of the most closely watched journeys in recent criminal justice history.

FBI surveillance teams tracked Kohberger for four days before his arrest, while law enforcement worked with prosecutors to develop enough probable cause to obtain a warrant. This wasn't a simple local police operation—it required coordination between multiple FBI field offices, state police agencies, and federal prosecutors to ensure the surveillance was both legal and effective.

The cross-country drive itself became part of the evidence against Kohberger. He drove cross-country in his white

Hyundai Elantra and arrived at his parents' house in Pennsylvania around Christmas. During this journey, he was pulled over twice by Indiana State Police within minutes of each other—once for speeding and once for following too closely. What Kohberger likely didn't know was that these traffic stops weren't random.

Law enforcement sources later revealed that Kohberger was stopped at the request of an FBI surveillance team that was following him to check for signs of hand injuries following the violent killings. The officers were specifically looking for any visible wounds that might corroborate the prosecution's theory that he had been involved in a violent struggle during the murders. While no significant injuries were documented during these stops, the fact that law enforcement was already tracking him demonstrated how quickly the investigation had focused on him as the primary suspect.

The surveillance operation was extraordinarily complex. FBI surveillance teams had to coordinate across multiple states, with teams handing off responsibility as Kohberger crossed jurisdictional boundaries. This type of interstate surveillance requires significant resources and legal coordination, indicating that law enforcement was confident they had identified their suspect.

During the surveillance period, investigators were also working on a parallel track to gather additional evidence. On December 27, 2022, Pennsylvania law enforcement collected trash from outside the Kohberger family home in Albrightsville. The Idaho State Lab determined that DNA found in this trash likely belonged to the biological father of the person who left DNA on the knife sheath, with at least 99.9998% of the male population expected to be excluded from the possibility of being the suspect's biological father.

This trash collection was crucial because it provided investigators with a comparison sample that could link Kohberger to the crime scene DNA without requiring his direct cooperation. The fact that the familial DNA match was so strong gave investigators the final piece they needed to justify an arrest warrant.

December 30, 2022: The Arrest That Shocked the Nation

At approximately 3:00 AM on December 30, 2022, the largest murder investigation in Idaho's recent history reached its dramatic conclusion. Pennsylvania State Police tactical teams surrounded the Kohberger family home in Albrightsville, a small community in the Pocono Mountains, preparing to arrest the man they believed was responsible for the Idaho student murders.

The arrest required tactical assets to be staged throughout Monroe County on the evening of December 29, with the actual arrest executed in the early hours of December 30. Pennsylvania State Police Major Christopher Paris explained that the arrest was conducted before dawn because Kohberger's warrant merited an after-dark arrest, which requires a higher standard of probable cause but allows for greater operational security.

When officers entered the home, they found Kohberger in his parents' kitchen wearing latex medical gloves and sorting trash into separate ziplock bags. This scene was particularly striking to investigators—here was a criminology PhD student who appeared to be taking precautions against leaving forensic evidence even in his own family's home. His behavior suggested an awareness of how DNA and trace evidence could be used in criminal investigations.

The arrest itself was conducted without incident, but the preparation had been extensive. The tactical response team had reviewed floor plans of the home and was prepared to break multiple doors and windows if necessary. The level of preparation reflected law enforcement's concern about arresting a suspect who had allegedly committed such violent crimes and who had academic knowledge of police procedures.

What made the arrest particularly dramatic was Kohberger's apparent calm demeanor. According to his attorney, Jason LaBar, Kohberger's family was "shocked" by the arrest and believed police had "nabbed the wrong man." LaBar described the family's reaction, saying they were awakened by FBI agents, local police, and Idaho State Troopers at approximately 3 AM, creating a scene of "shock and awe".

The timing of the arrest was carefully calculated. Investigators had waited until they had overwhelming evidence—the genetic genealogy identification, the DNA match from the family's trash, the cell phone data, and the surveillance footage. But they also couldn't wait much longer, as Kohberger was scheduled to return to Washington State University for the spring semester, which would have required coordinating the arrest across multiple states and potentially alerting him to the investigation.

The arrest made national headlines within hours. The University of Idaho murders had captivated the country for seven weeks, with daily speculation about when police would identify a suspect. The revelation that the alleged perpetrator was a criminology PhD student studying at a nearby university added a layer of irony and intrigue that captured public imagination.

For the families of Kaylee Goncalves, Madison Mogen, Xana Kernodle, and Ethan Chapin, the arrest represented a crucial step toward justice, though their ordeal was far from over. The investigation had demonstrated how modern forensic techniques—genetic genealogy, digital forensics, and sophisticated surveillance—could solve even the most challenging cases. But it also raised questions about privacy, the limits of police surveillance, and the ethical implications of using consumer DNA databases for criminal investigations.

As Kohberger was led away in handcuffs, the most intensive murder investigation in Idaho's history entered a new phase. The hunt for the killer was over, but the pursuit of justice was just beginning.

Chapter 8: Trial by Media and Law - The Path to Justice

When Bryan Kohberger's probable cause affidavit was unsealed on January 5, 2023, the document revealed the methodical investigation that had led to his arrest six days earlier. The 19-page document laid out a compelling case built on DNA evidence, digital forensics, and eyewitness testimony that would become the foundation for one of the most high-profile murder trials in recent memory.

The affidavit revealed that investigators had linked Kohberger to the crime scene through a "tan leather knife sheath" found next to Madison Mogen's body, which contained DNA that would ultimately be traced back to him. The sheath bore the markings "Ka-bar" and "USMC" along with the U.S. Marine Corps insignia, providing investigators with crucial physical evidence that had been left behind in what otherwise appeared to be a carefully planned attack.

The DNA breakthrough came through innovative investigative genetic genealogy work. When Kohberger's DNA profile didn't match anyone in the FBI's CODIS database, investigators recovered trash from the Kohberger family residence in Pennsylvania on December 27, 2022. The Idaho State Lab determined that the DNA from the family's trash most likely belonged to the biological father of the person whose DNA was found on the knife sheath, with statistical analysis showing that "at least 99.9998% of the male population would be expected to be excluded from the possibility of being the suspect's biological father".

The affidavit also revealed the extensive digital surveillance that had helped investigators track Kohberger's movements. Cell phone records showed that Kohberger's phone had been in the area of the victims' home on at least twelve occasions prior to November 13, 2022, with all but one of these visits occurring during late evening and early morning hours. On the night of the murders, his phone went silent from approximately 2:47 AM until 4:48 AM, covering the crucial time frame when the killings occurred.

Perhaps most chillingly, the document revealed that a surviving roommate, identified as D.M., had seen a masked figure "clad in black clothing" walking past her bedroom door toward the back exit. Her description of the intruder as approximately 6 feet tall with an athletic build and "bushy eyebrows" would prove remarkably consistent with Kohberger's physical appearance.

The surveillance evidence was equally damning. Video footage from the area showed a white Hyundai Elantra making multiple passes by the victims' home between 3:29 AM and 4:20 AM, with the vehicle ultimately departing "at a high rate of speed". Investigators would later determine this vehicle belonged to Kohberger, who had suspiciously changed his license plates from Pennsylvania to Washington just five days after the murders.

The affidavit painted a picture of methodical surveillance followed by a brutal attack. Kohberger had allegedly spent thirty minutes circling the victims' home before entering, making three initial passes before finally approaching the house around 4:04 AM. The timing was particularly significant, as it occurred just minutes after Xana Kernodle had received a DoorDash delivery, suggesting the killer may have been waiting for the house to settle into silence.

Legal Maneuvering: Defense Strategies and Prosecution Response

As Kohberger's trial date approached, both the defense and prosecution engaged in complex legal maneuvering that would shape how the case would be presented to a jury. The defense team, led by public defender Anne Taylor, faced the daunting task of defending against what appeared to be overwhelming physical and digital evidence while the prosecution prepared to seek the death penalty.

The defense has asked the court to limit the use of inflammatory language at trial, including restrictions on the word "murder" and banning terms like "psychopath," "sociopath," and even references to Kohberger's "bushy eyebrows". They've also requested limitations on crime scene photos, arguing that too many grisly images could be "inflammatory" and violate Kohberger's right to a fair trial.

In one of the most consequential motions, Kohberger's defense has asked the court to throw out the possibility of the death penalty on grounds that prosecutors took too long handing over discovery disclosures. Defense attorney Anne Taylor has argued that the massive volume of digital evidence, which she claims could take up to three years to properly review, has created an impossible timeline for adequate preparation.

The defense has also pursued an "alternate perpetrator" strategy, though details remain sealed by the court. Judge Steven Hippler is set to consider a defense request to allow them to introduce evidence of an "alternate perpetrator" in the killings, with the judge having sealed the details of this defense request. This strategy suggests the defense may argue that someone else committed the murders, despite the DNA evidence linking Kohberger to the scene.

Defense attorney Anne Taylor has told the court that she would need more time to process additional discovery and get a new defense witness up to speed after a previous one died. She has consistently argued that the defense team is not prepared for trial, citing the enormous volume of evidence that includes what she describes as "68 terabytes of information to review."

The prosecution, meanwhile, has pushed back against defense delay tactics. Special deputy prosecutor Joshua Hurwit has accused Kohberger's defense team of using a "scorched earth" strategy, arguing that "the record supports denying the motion based on what the defense has been doing, continues to do, and will continue to do". Prosecutors have maintained their intent to seek the death penalty and have expressed confidence in their evidence.

The prosecution has also had to contend with unauthorized media leaks that have complicated their case preparation. Information shared during a "Dateline" episode included surveillance video and FBI cell phone tower data that prosecutors argue must have come from unauthorized sources within the investigation. This has led to concerns about information security and potential contempt charges for those responsible for the leaks.

The decision to move Kohberger's trial from Latah County to Ada County represented a significant development in the case, reflecting concerns about the intense media coverage and the difficulty of finding impartial jurors in the small college town where the murders occurred.

The previous judge granted a request from Kohberger's lawyers to move the trial venue to Boise, Idaho's capital, about 300 miles away from Latah County, citing potential bias in jury selection if the trial were held in Moscow. The small college town of Moscow, with a population of approximately 25,000, had been completely transformed by the murders and the subsequent investigation.

The venue change brought the case under the jurisdiction of Ada County District Court Judge Steven Hippler, who has implemented strict guidelines for the high-profile proceedings. Rules for the upcoming proceedings stipulate that the trial will be livestreamed, though close-up shots are prohibited, and video feeds will be cut when surviving roommates testify.

Due to extensive media coverage and logistical challenges, the judge has instituted strict guidelines on courtroom access and electronic device use, with one seat reserved daily for a pooled journalist from Latah County to share coverage with other outlets, while general attendance will be controlled through an online ticketing system.

The logistical challenges of the venue change have been significant. The trial's relocation far from Moscow has created difficulties for witnesses, victims' families, and community members who have been following the case closely. However, legal experts have generally supported the decision, recognizing that finding an impartial jury in Moscow would have been nearly impossible given the case's impact on the small community.

The trial is scheduled to begin on August 11, 2025, and continue through November 7, 2025, including two weeks of jury selection, eight weeks of the trial itself, and potentially additional time for penalty phase proceedings if Kohberger is convicted. The extended timeline reflects both the complexity of the case and the thoroughness required in death penalty proceedings.

The Documentary Phenomenon: "One Night in Idaho" and Media Impact

The upcoming Amazon Prime Video documentary "One Night in Idaho: The College Murders" has become a significant factor in the legal proceedings, with defense attorneys arguing that its release so close to the trial date could prejudice potential jurors and complicate the pursuit of justice.

"One Night in Idaho: The College Murders" is a four-part documentary series directed and produced by Liz Garbus and Matthew Galkin, scheduled to premiere on July 11, 2025, on Amazon Prime Video. The series centers on the families and friends of the victims, featuring exclusive interviews with Stacey and Jim Chapin (parents of Ethan Chapin) and Karen and Scott Laramie (parents of Madison Mogen).

The documentary has created significant legal complications for the upcoming trial. Defense attorney Anne Taylor argued that a recent Dateline special, along with the upcoming docuseries and related book releases, could complicate jury selection, stating "The moment we start attempting to select a jury in this case, those things are going to be on everybody's TV, everybody's social media feed".

Kohberger's attorney has argued that media coverage, including the Amazon Prime docuseries "One Night in Idaho," coming out on July 11, is causing issues with the fairness of the upcoming trial. The defense has requested a trial delay based partly on this media coverage, though Judge Hippler indicated he likely won't delay the August trial, stating "it's likely you're going to trial on the date indicated".

The documentary represents a broader phenomenon in true crime media, where major cases receive extensive coverage while legal proceedings are still ongoing. Directors Liz Garbus and Matthew Galkin are known for their ethical approach to true crime, with both filmmakers having worked on projects that center around ethical considerations and highlighting stories of marginalized people often ignored by media and police.

For the families, the documentary provides an opportunity to control their narrative. As director Liz Garbus explained, "What is the side that is untold? At the end of the day, these kids are victims. And their families deserve their stories to be told in fulsome, loving ways". The series aims to move beyond the social media speculation and conspiracy theories that dominated early coverage of the case.

However, the timing has created a legal dilemma. The prosecution has expressed frustration with the defense's request for delays based on media coverage, with the prosecutor arguing "Every time there's a breaking story, every time there's a new book or a new documentary, are we going to continue the trial indefinitely?"

Throughout the legal proceedings, the families of Madison Mogen, Kaylee Goncalves, Xana Kernodle, and Ethan Chapin have become powerful voices advocating for justice while working to preserve the memory of their loved ones beyond the tragedy that took their lives.

In the upcoming documentary, Hunter Chapin, Ethan's brother, recalled the fear and uncertainty following the killings: "There's this person out there who had just murdered our brother and he's still out there somewhere". This statement captures the emotional toll the prolonged investigation and legal proceedings have taken on the families.

The Chapin family has been particularly vocal about their experience navigating the media circus that surrounded the case. In conversations with the documentary filmmakers, the Chapins described "being swept up in this circus from the inside," dealing with TikTok videos and hypothesizing that had their son's name "dragged through the mud unfairly" when none of the conspiracy theories turned out to be true.

Kaylee Goncalves' father, Steve Goncalves, has been one of the most outspoken family members throughout the process. He has conducted his own investigation, hired private investigators, and frequently spoken to the media about his frustration with the pace of the legal proceedings. His advocacy has kept public attention focused on the case while also raising questions about the balance between family activism and the legal process.

The families have had to navigate the unique challenges of a social media age, where their children's deaths became the subject of endless online speculation and amateur detective work. As filmmaker Matthew Galkin noted, "Major crime in

2025 has all of these layers of attention and social media and speculation where that didn't exist a few decades ago, but now it's what all of these families have to deal with on a daily basis".

Beyond seeking justice through the legal system, the families have worked to establish lasting memorials for their children. The University of Idaho created scholarships in the victims' names, while the Chapin family established the "Ethan's Smile" foundation. These efforts represent their determination to ensure their children are remembered for their lives rather than just their deaths.

The families have also had to cope with the prolonged legal process, including multiple delays and venue changes. The emotional toll of waiting for justice while dealing with continued media attention and legal proceedings has been significant, with some family members expressing frustration at the length of time between the murders and the trial.

Preparing for Trial: The Case That Will Define Modern Forensics

As the August 2025 trial date approaches, the Bryan Kohberger case is positioned to become a landmark proceeding that will demonstrate the power of modern forensic science while testing the limits of digital privacy and investigative techniques in criminal justice.

The case represents a convergence of cutting-edge investigative methods that may set precedents for future prosecutions. The use of investigative genetic genealogy, extensive cell phone data analysis, and sophisticated surveillance footage interpretation has created what legal experts consider one of the most technologically advanced criminal cases in recent history.

The prosecution believes it will take roughly a month and a half to present their case, while the defense will need an additional four weeks to present their arguments. If a jury finds Kohberger guilty, the penalty phase of the trial could take an additional three weeks, reflecting the thorough process required in death penalty cases.

The DNA evidence will likely be central to the prosecution's case, with the knife sheath providing what appears to be definitive physical evidence linking Kohberger to the crime scene. However, the defense is expected to challenge both the collection methods and the interpretation of the genetic genealogy work that led to Kohberger's identification.

The digital evidence presents both opportunities and challenges for both sides. The extensive cell phone data and surveillance footage provide a detailed timeline of Kohberger's movements, but the defense may argue that correlation doesn't prove causation and that being in the area doesn't constitute proof of murder.

A new potential witness has emerged in the form of a DoorDash driver who appears to say she saw Kohberger at the scene, though her testimony may be complicated by her admission to taking prescription medication and her emotional state during police interviews. This witness could provide crucial eyewitness testimony linking Kohberger to the scene at the time of the murders.

The trial will also test the limits of media coverage in high-profile cases. The proceedings will be livestreamed with restrictions, and the judge has implemented strict guidelines about courtroom access and electronic device use. The balance between public access to justice and protecting the integrity of the proceedings will be closely watched by legal observers.

The case has already influenced how law enforcement approaches major investigations, particularly in the use of genetic genealogy and digital forensics. The successful identification of Kohberger through these methods has validated their use while raising important questions about privacy rights and the extent of law enforcement's reach in the digital age.

As the legal teams make their final preparations, the Kohberger trial is poised to become a defining moment in modern criminal justice, demonstrating both the power and the limitations of 21st-century forensic science in the pursuit of justice for Madison Mogen, Kaylee Goncalves, Xana Kernodle, and Ethan Chapin.

Conclusion: Legacy of a Tragedy - How Four Lives Lost Changed Criminal Justice Forever

It's remarkable how a single, devastating event, particularly one involving the loss of innocent lives, can send ripples through a society, eventually reaching the very foundations of its legal and justice systems. We often see criminal justice as this rigid, established structure, but history shows us it's constantly evolving, often in response to these profound tragedies. When we talk about "four lives lost changing criminal justice forever," we're delving into a powerful narrative about how sorrow, public outcry, and the relentless pursuit of answers can reshape the very mechanisms designed to protect us and deliver fairness.

Think about it this way: for every intricate law, for every protocol police follow, for every right an accused person has, there's usually a story behind it, often a painful one. These aren't just abstract legal concepts; they are often etched in the memory of real human suffering. While I can't point to one specific, universally recognized case of "four lives lost" that singularly changed criminal justice in every jurisdiction, we can examine the types of tragedies that have historically driven significant reform.

One of the most profound shifts has come from cases where the justice system itself was perceived to have failed, either in preventing the crime, apprehending the right perpetrator, or ensuring a just process. Take, for instance, instances of wrongful convictions. When an innocent person spends years, or even decades, behind bars for a crime they didn't commit, and this miscarriage of justice is eventually exposed, it doesn't just impact that individual. It erodes public trust and forces a deep, uncomfortable look at the system's flaws.

Consider the rise of DNA evidence. Before its widespread use, convictions often relied heavily on eyewitness testimony, confessions (which could sometimes be coerced), and circumstantial evidence. When DNA began to exonerate individuals who had been wrongly convicted, sometimes even those on death row, it was a stark, undeniable demonstration of systemic fallibility. This wasn't about one mistake; it was about a pattern that indicated fundamental issues with investigative techniques and trial procedures. The loss of years, the loss of freedom, and in some cases, the loss of life itself for those executed before their innocence was proven, created an undeniable moral imperative for change.

The push for better forensic science, stricter rules around interrogations, and the widespread adoption of post-conviction DNA testing in many places are direct legacies of these revealed injustices. It's not just about getting the "bad guy"; it's about ensuring the "right guy" is indeed the bad guy. These reforms came from the recognition that the price of error was too high, measured in human lives and shattered families.

Another area where tragedy has spurred immense change is in victim's rights. For a long time, victims of crime were often sidelined in the criminal justice process. Their voices were rarely heard in court beyond their testimony, and their needs – emotional, financial, or informational – were often overlooked. However, a series of particularly brutal or high-profile crimes, often involving the loss of multiple lives, began to galvanize movements for greater victim participation and support.

The concept of Victim Impact Statements (VIS), for example, gained traction largely due to the tireless advocacy of victims' families. Imagine a family reeling from the unimaginable loss of their loved ones. They go through the court process, see the perpetrator convicted, but feel a profound sense of incompleteness. They want the court to understand the true depth of their suffering, not just the legal facts of the case. The ability to present a Victim Impact Statement, allowing those directly affected to articulate the profound personal, emotional, and financial toll of the crime, was a monumental shift. It humanized the legal proceedings, reminding everyone involved that behind the case numbers and legal jargon were real people whose lives were irrevocably altered. This change wasn't just symbolic; it influenced sentencing decisions and parole hearings, ensuring the victim's experience was a tangible factor in the administration of justice.

Furthermore, these tragedies often expose gaps in legislation or societal protections. We've seen how horrific events involving domestic violence, hate crimes, or school shootings have prompted intense public debate and led to the creation of new laws, enhanced penalties, or preventative measures. Each time, the focus shifts from "how could this happen?" to "how can we prevent this from happening again?" This often involves scrutinizing existing laws, identifying weaknesses, and advocating for changes that, while perhaps not bringing back the lost lives, aim to safeguard future ones.

Consider the ongoing evolution of police reform, particularly in response to instances of excessive force or misconduct that have led to fatalities. When these events come to light, often amplified by media and social activism, they spark profound questions about accountability, training, and community relations. While these reforms are complex and ongoing, the impetus for change often stems from the tragic loss of life and the subsequent demand for systemic transformation to prevent similar future occurrences. The conversation moves beyond individual culpability to the broader practices and culture within law enforcement.

In essence, while the term "four lives lost" might not refer to a singular, named event that universally reshaped criminal justice, it represents the collective weight of countless individual tragedies. Each instance where lives are brutally taken, especially in circumstances that highlight systemic failings, serves as a powerful, albeit painful, catalyst for change. These losses force us to confront uncomfortable truths about our society and our justice system. They fuel advocacy, spark legislative action, and ultimately, leave a lasting legacy on how we define justice, protect our communities, and strive to prevent future sorrow. The journey is never truly over, but each tragedy, in its own way, contributes to the ongoing, often difficult, but ultimately essential, evolution of criminal justice.

Printed in Dunstable, United Kingdom